Assessing
Differentiated
Student
Products

Assessing Differentiated Student Products

A Protocol for Development and Evaluation

Julia L. Roberts, Ed.D.
and Tracy F. Inman

PRUFROCK PRESS INC.
WACO, TEXAS

Roberts, Julia L. (Julia Link)
  Assessing differentiated student products : a protocol for development and assessment / Julia L. Roberts, Tracy F. Inman.
    p. cm.
  ISBN-13: 978-1-59363-355-4 (pbk.)
  ISBN-10: 1-59363-355-6 (pbk.)
  1. Academic achievement—Evaluation. 2. Learning—Evaluation. 3. Educational tests and measurements. I. Inman, Tracy F. (Tracy Ford), 1963– II. Title.
  LB3051.R577 2009
  371.26'2—dc22
                        2008034166

Edited by Jennifer Robins
Production Design by Marjorie Parker

ISBN-13: 978-1-59363-355-4
ISBN-10: 1-59363-355-6

Prufrock Press Inc.
P.O. Box 8813
Waco, TX 76714-8813
Phone: (800) 998-2208
Fax: (800) 240-0333
http://www.prufrock.com

Contents

List of Figures

Acknowledgements

A very special thank you goes to Gail Hiles whose creativity, design skills, and tireless dedication made this book and its many figures possible. For their expert insight and generous giving of time, we'd like to thank the following people for assistance with individual DAP Tools: Corey Alderdice, Miwon Choe, Robert Forsythe, Chris Joffrion, Paul Johnson, Jana Kirchner, Tony Kirchner, Keith Lancaster, Judy Pierce, Nancy Rice, Rico Tyler, and Renee Watkins. We also greatly appreciate Lynette Baldwin for her careful reading of our text and her invaluable suggestions.

Chapter 1

Developing and Assessing Products

Have you ever wished for an assessment that works for many different assignments? Have you wanted a ready guide for developing and assessing products—a variety of products? If you answered "yes" to either of these questions, then the DAP Tool is for you! The DAP Tool (DAP stands for Developing and Assessing Products) is a protocol that, when adopted by a single teacher or entire district, simplifies the assessment process, encourages differentiation, and takes the ceiling off of learning.

This book is all about assessment, specifically *the assessment of student performance and learning that occurs while students are developing products.* In this book, *the goal of assessment is to guide learning.* For children to learn on an ongoing basis, assessment must be ongoing as well. Assessment also must be consistent across assignments and disciplines if it is to be useful in facilitating learning. The DAP Tool is a vehicle that consistently guides the development and assessment of products and promotes learning.

Now, let's look at products and what they can accomplish. What do a podcast, technical report, monologue, and poster have in common when they are the end products of assignments or units? All are designed to communicate information and/or demonstrate skills. Besides being a vehicle for communication and skill demonstration, the second commonality is that not only can a podcast, technical report, monologue, and poster be classroom assignments, but they also are products used by professionals outside the school environment. They are assignments with a future. Young people recognize that these products have relevance in the world beyond the classroom. Each product shares the goal of communicating important ideas in skillful ways to a target audience, but how each product looks and what is communicated and/or demonstrated vary widely. Target audiences even differ from product to product. Just like professional products, school products must meet high standards if they are to be effective in communicating ideas and demonstrating skills to a specific audience.

What exactly is a product then? *Products are vehicles for communicating information and/or demonstrating skills for specific purposes to authentic audiences.* In school, the product communicates information and/or demonstrates skills to you, the teacher, or to you plus another audience (hopefully, a real-world audience). In various professions, products are used to communicate information as well, once again to an audience specific to the job or position (an authentic audience). For example, a marketing director pitches an idea to a client through a PowerPoint presentation, an architect communicates a design via a blueprint, and a travel agent creates a brochure for an upcoming cruise. In the world of work, products are an integral part of many professions.

Products provide you with tremendous opportunities to differentiate instruction and facilitate continuous progress. *Differentiated learning experiences* vary the content, process, product, and/or assessment in order to address the needs, interests, abilities, and readiness levels of students. The goal of differentiating instruction is to promote continuous progress. *Continuous progress* is learning that is ongoing. Continuous progress occurs when young people have opportunities to learn new content and skills every day. Indeed, the DAP Tool can guide you as you plan and implement differentiated learning experiences.

The following eight reasons tell why products are important in classrooms. They explain why products and the assessment of products are so central to learning that they become the focus of an entire book.

- *Products are engaging.* Products involve students in hands-on, minds-on learning experiences. Products require young people to do something and to become actively involved with the content as they are learning. They make learning enjoyable, even fun.

- *Products are motivating.* The wide range of products makes it possible to get students learning content that may hold little interest for them until they have the opportunity to develop products in which they have high interest. For example, an artistic child who isn't very interested in history may engage in the study wholeheartedly if he knows he'll be able to show what he's learned through a painting or sculpture. Products provide the hook that brings children into active learning.

- *Products have "real-world" connections.* Products are important in the world beyond school. The carry-over from academic work to life is motivating as it provides purpose. Products have a future beyond academics. They add relevance to learning experiences.

- *Well-developed products require high-level thinking and problem-solving skills.* They engage students in thinking in new ways about the content being studied. Expectations for high-level thinking and problem solving add rigor and complexity to learning experiences. Thinking and problem solving are keys to success in the 21st century.

- *Products provide a practical way for teachers to match learning experiences to students' preferred ways of learning.* Such a match increases both motivation and task commitment. A child who loves technology will be more likely to work hard when he has opportunities to work on products that include technology. The same is true with kinesthetic, oral, visual, and written preferences for learning.

- *Products allow for and encourage self-expression and creativity.* Self-expression and creativity personalize the learning of content for young people. Products in one assignment will not duplicate each other when self-expression is encouraged. For example, an entire classroom of posters would differ from each other because of the personal insight and creative spark included in each. That is an advantage to both you and the students, as assessing products is more rewarding when they show self-expression and are not cookie-cutter versions of the same product.

- *Products foster pride in one's work.* Students are proud when they create a product that requires their best efforts. Expectations must be high, but not too high for the student to meet them. Creating high-level products builds self-confidence, and self-confidence nurtures a desire to rise to the next level of accomplishment.

- *Products develop lifelong learners.* As students become interested in content via the products they create, they ask questions that lead to new learning. They see connections between concepts within and among courses. They establish patterns of learning. Learning becomes a habit and a passion. Reflecting on learning when a product has been completed leads to asking new questions about the topic and encourages lifelong learning.

If these eight reasons resonate with you, keep reading. This book addresses ways to make authentic assessment, significant content, creativity, and reflection central to the discussion of products. These important concepts come together in the DAP Tool, a protocol for developing and assessing content, creativity, reflection, and, of course, the product itself.

One strength of the DAP Tool is its consistency. Every single product, regardless of subject area or content, will be developed and assessed by the same four components: Content, Presentation, Creativity, and Reflection. In fact, even the criteria and descriptors for three of the four components are the same; only Presentation differs because it is specific to each individual product. (Don't worry, you'll understand fully once you read Chapter 3.) Another strength is that the varying tiers of expectations (there are three for every single product) allow for ease in differentiating. Each tier increases in sophistication so that once you match the appropriate tier to the student, you have a consistent, reliable protocol for differentiating (Chapter 4 will guide you through that). And finally, this tool will encourage you to remove the learning ceiling in that the Performance Scale doesn't top out at proficiency or even one level beyond. This scale encourages learners to challenge themselves. (Again, Chapter 4 will explain this in more detail.) From ways to develop and organize product lists (Chapter 2) to methods for implementing the DAP Tool in an educational setting (Chapter 5), this book will guide you from start to finish. For those of you who want a dependable way to guide students in developing products, you will find the DAP Tool incredibly useful. (And, Chapter 6 provides a plethora of DAP Tools for products to suit all learning preferences!) For those of you who have been searching for continuity, reliability, and ease in assessing student products, the DAP Tool is what you've been looking for.

Chapter 2

Products

Making Learning Real

Podcast. Technical report. Interview. Model. Interpretive dance. Learners have myriad ways to demonstrate the content they've learned. The traditional pen-and-paper multiple-choice and short-essay test, although a valid assessment, is not the only viable option when it comes to determining the complexity and depth of content learned. Take the states of matter, for example. How can a student show you, the teacher, what he knows about the states of matter? Could he design and develop a podcast using the characteristics and examples of the states of matter as his content? Sure, he could. What about writing a technical report? Yes. Could he interview an expert in science about the topic? Of course. What about creating a 3-D model focusing on molecules of the three states of matter? You bet. An interpretive dance on the three states of matter? For someone who is gifted and talented in dance, this is a wonderful option! Just imagine the changing tempo and movement as she becomes molecules. When learning the content is more important than the product, intentionally providing product options proves an ideal way to meet the needs, interests, and abilities of your students.

Although products are used to demonstrate what the student knows, products also are important on their own. An accomplished scientist must know the components of a technical report as well as an experiment. The writer must understand the differences between formal and informal pieces of writing and the roles audience and purpose play. We must teach products. A student can't create a monologue until she knows what one is, and she can't produce one of excellence unless she understands what that looks like. Professionals are not only experts in their content, but they also are experts in the way the content is presented (i.e., the product). Therefore, an architect must master the components of a blueprint and a model. A politician must know how to write and give effective speeches. A journalist must hone the art of interviewing and writing. Each profession calls for specific products. Rarely in adult life are we faced with multiple-choice and short-answer options! Products, then, provide a way to authentically assess what has been learned.

Authentic assessment proves critical. When we provide choice in those authentic assessments, we better meet our students' needs, and we also may pique their interest. If a student has a product choice that intrigues her (e.g., technology), she may well be enticed to study a content area that doesn't interest her. It may be worth her while to ponder the causes of the French Revolution if she can portray those thoughts through a PowerPoint presentation incorporating movie clips and colorful charts instead of a pen-and-paper assignment or test. Likewise, a gifted young artist may relish the thought of an "end-of-unit exam" that is really a series of political cartoons analyzing the cultural, economic, and political causes of the revolution. Chances are that, if motivation and interest are present in the student, his end product will be a better assessment of the knowledge he gained. And in the real world, professionals really do create PowerPoints and political cartoons.

Key to this concept is authentic assessment—not only does that mean real-world products, but it also implies that the product be assessed authentically. That means that each unique component of the product (i.e., what makes the product the product) should be addressed. For example, if a student creates a pamphlet, then graphics, text, and layout all need to be assessed. The components of a model are its construction, realistic representation, and labeling, so each of these areas needs to be examined. Each product has specific components inherent in its nature; therefore, an authentic assessment of a product must examine each component. (For a full explanation of the components of any product, see Chapter 3.) Your students—in addition to you—need to understand what must be in place for a specific product. That's why our model is called DAP Tool—it means Developing and Assessing Products Tool. Both the student and the teacher utilize the tool: It guides the student as she creates the product just as it guides the educator as he assesses the product.

Categories

Not only is it important to provide a variety of choices when it comes to product, but it also is critical to make those choices intentional. Don't just give a random list of options. For example, if you know that the unit will take 2 days, do you really want to provide choices that will take 3 weeks to complete? Likewise, if you teach in a school with a very high poverty rate, do you want to include products that require many supplies and expensive materials? Do you want to provide only written choices or only oral ones? The list of products you supply to your class must be intentional and deliberately composed.

So, how do you create the list of products?

- *Step 1.* Think about instructional intent. Are you trying to address all learning preferences or multiple intelligences? If so, then include products that match each learning preference or each intelligence. (Lazear's *The Rubrics Way: Using Multiple Intelligences to Assess Understanding* [1998] provides excellent choices.) Perhaps you are concerned about part-to-whole relationships or even abstract versus concrete thinking. If so, arrange your lists accordingly. Perhaps you want to provide options for both group and individual products. Instructional intent should help dictate the list.

- *Step 2.* Consider your physical parameters. If time is important, only suggest those products that fit into your time frame. Likewise, if cost and availability of supplies are issues, select those products for which you can provide all necessary materials and resources.

- *Step 3.* And, lastly, of course, you always have to consider the grading. Do you have a scoring guide for each product listed? That's a must. Of course, if you utilize DAP Tools, you have a plethora of rubrics right at your fingertips. If you don't, then you must be sure to have rubrics ready for any product choice you offer.

Taking instructional intent, physical parameters, and assessment into consideration, you are ready to create the product list. You can categorize the product list in myriad ways (from learning preference to availability of supplies)—just be sure that each list for each assignment is thoughtfully constructed.

Without thoughtful consideration, we may unintentionally limit students. Consider the English teacher who, thinking herself progressive, gave choices of product: essay, short story, poem—as long as it was written, it was fine with her. After all, writing and reading were her areas of expertise, her comfort zones. Think of how many learning styles she ignored. What about those students who learned kinesthetically? Orally? What about those who were musically inclined? The wonderful thing about giving intentional choices of products is that the teacher can address specific learning styles. In fact, when you examine the product resources available, most of them categorize according to learning style. This type of categorization is applicable to any classroom, any content, and any ability level.

For example, Karnes and Stephens (2000) divided their book on developing products into five categories: visual, oral, performance, written, and multicategorical. Curry and Samara (1991) developed their Curriculum Project materials according to kinesthetic, oral, visual, and written divisions. Coil (2004) also categorized her products based on learning preference: visual, verbal, kinesthetic, and technological. You may choose to use Dunn and Dunn (2003); Silver, Strong, and Perini (2000); or any of the many others available. Whatever the template, categorizing products according to learning style assists in differentiation because students tend to select those products in their comfort zone of learning.

Based on learning styles, DAP Tools are categorized into five main areas: kinesthetic, oral, technological, visual, and written.

Kinesthetic

Kinesthetic products are those that require hands-on involvement. Kinesthetic learners typically involve the whole body when learning. Lamarche-Bisson (2002) explained:

> The kinesthetic learner should be encouraged to use his need for movement productively. . . . By representing what he has learned through an experiment (science), with a model or a graph (math), or in a mime or skit (drama), the kinesthetic learner could demonstrate what he has understood and retained. (p. 268)

Other products include dances, demonstrations, inventions, paintings, sculptures, and service-learning projects.

Oral

Oral learners tend to rely on nonwritten methods of learning. They thrive with class discussion and group work, and learn best by listening (Vincent & Ross, 2001). Oral learners, then, favor products that focus on the verbal. Sample products include debates, interviews, monologues, newscasts, oral presentations, radio advertisements, songs, and speeches.

Technological

Many learners thrive on technology and would choose some sort of technology as their preferred way of learning and demonstrating what they've learned. A simple Google search for "learning through technology" creates 15 million hits! Technology may be difficult to separate from other areas because most products can be generated with some sort of technology (e.g., a word processing program for writing or producing a pamphlet). Products relying solely on technology are many: blogs, computer games, computer graphics, computer programs, documentaries, podcasts, PowerPoint presentations, movies, Web pages, and wikis.

Visual

Someone who learns visually tends to learn best through images such as illustrations, diagrams, graphs, and flow charts. They typically think in pictures, relying on symbols, color, and white space when learning (VARK, 2007). So, products that best demonstrate their learning include cartoons, charts, collages, exhibits, graphic organizers, pamphlets, and posters.

Written

These learners prefer reading and writing. They tend "to take information most efficiently from reading headings, lists, definitions, lecture-notes, and textbooks" (Zapalska & Brozik, 2006, p. 329). In fact, they frequently convert other forms of information into the written word. Products best suited for them include diaries, essays, feature articles, letters, newsletters, poems, reviews, and technical reports (see Figure 2.1 for a more complete listing of products).

Products With
More Than One Category

Some products clearly seem to fall into a specific learning style category. For example, a speech and an interview are oral products, just as an essay and short story are written products. Or are they? What if that speech had

Advertisement/PSA (print)	Feature Article	Photo
Advertisement (radio)	Game	Photo Essay
Advertisement (television)	Graph	Plan
Audiotape	Graphic Organizer	Play
Biography	Greeting Card	Podcast
Blog	Illustrated Story	Poem
Blueprint	Illustration	Political Cartoon
Book	Interview (live)	Poster
Book Cover	Interview (recorded)	PowerPoint Presentation
Bulletin Board	Interview (written)	Project
Cartoon	Invention	PSA (radio)
Case Study	Lesson	PSA (television)
Chart	Letter (business)	Puppet
Choral Reading	Letter (friendly)	Puppet Show
Collage	Letter to Editor	Questionnaire
Collection	Mask	Research Report
Column	Matrix	Review
Computer Graphic	Mentorship	Science Fair Project
Computer Program	Mime	Sculpture
Costume	Mock Trial (attorney)	Scrapbook
Dance	Mock Trial (defendant)	Script
Debate	Mock Trial (judge)	Service-Learning Project
Demonstration	Mock Trial (plaintiff)	Skit
Diagram	Model	Song
Dialogue	Monologue	Speech (oral)
Diary/Journal	Movie	Speech (written)
Diorama	Mural	Story
Document-Based Question	Museum Exhibit	Story Telling
Documentary	Musical	Survey
Dramatic Presentation	Newscast	Technical Report
Drawing	Newsletter	Timeline
Editorial	Newspaper Article	Venn Diagram
Essay	Open Response	Video Game
Exhibit/Display	Oral Report/ Presentation	Web Page
Experiment	Outline	Wiki
	Painting	Written Report
	Pamphlet/Brochure	

Figure 2.1. Product list.

to be written first? Then it no longer is simply an oral product—another element comes into play. What about the interview? Before you can simply categorize it as oral, you must take the following into account: Were the questions given to the student or did she have to compose them? Is it a live interview? A written one? One category simply might not explain it fully. For example, a cartoon is definitely visual—but if it has a caption, there is a written component as well. Most products, then, actually include more than one category.

Why is this important? Well, if your goal is differentiation through learning preferences, you must analyze each nuance of each product before offering it as a choice to your students. You need to realize that you may unintentionally limit some learners by listing too many products that mainly address one style while not listing or addressing any other style. Some authors such as Karnes and Stephens (2000) address this mixture of learning style by creating a multicategorical section. Although that acknowledgement is helpful, there is another approach.

PRIMARYsecondary

This simple approach is *PRIMARYsecondary*, an idea that played an important role in the development of the DAP Tool. In short, the primary learning style inherent in the product is represented by a capital letter. For example, the cartoon mentioned earlier is mainly visual, so it could be labeled with a capital V. Any secondary learning styles also present in the product are scripted with a lowercase letter. For instance, if that cartoon has a caption, then the secondary learning style (written) would be a lowercase w. Therefore, a captioned cartoon would be labeled Vw. An uncaptioned cartoon would be simply V (i.e., visual only as opposed to visual combined with written). Likewise, the interview mentioned earlier could be scripted in several ways depending on the type of interview. For example, an interview wherein the interviewer asks questions that are provided for him would be O (for oral). If he wrote the questions, then it would be Ow. A recorded interview could be either an O or an Ow (depending on who wrote the questions). However, a transcribed or written interview couldn't just be an O: It would have to be an Ow.

For the DAP Tool to be effective, one must look at the product closely when identifying style:

- If the product is primarily visual, but uses technology as well, then it would be labeled Vt (representing a primarily visual product with a secondary technological element).

- A presentation with an accompanying written piece would be Ow (for oral and written).

- A written product complete with a visual aid would be represented by Wv (meaning written plus visual), and

- A speech that includes a PowerPoint presentation would be categorized as Ot (for oral and technological).

Sometimes two letters aren't sufficient. A diorama, for example, could be Kv because it combines the kinesthetic with the visual element. The kinesthetic is the act of physically creating the diorama (e.g., cutting, gluing, etc.) using various materials in its representation. The visual element encompasses the artistic creation of the items in the diorama and the artwork involved. But, if that diorama also incorporates labeling or a written explanation, then another learning style—although minor—is addressed. So the product is then identified as Kvw (kinesthetic plus visual and written).

This method serves many purposes and is most beneficial when it is incorporated into the product list you distribute. First, it helps the student figure out the process of creating the product. For example, the diorama is primarily K when you consider the cutting, pasting, and placing—all the kinesthetic elements involved. But the visual element surfaces (i.e., Kv) as the learner considers color, space, shape, background, and artistic elements involved. Then the written aspect emerges (i.e., Kvw): He must label and perhaps explain the components used. As the learner looks at each letter, he acknowledges the multistep process involved in the creation of the diorama. In addition, the *PRIMARYsecondary* method encourages the student to think critically about her own learning. Not only is she cognizant of the steps involved in the process, she also becomes cognizant of her own preferences for learning. This encourages not only hands-on learning, but also, more importantly, minds-on learning. This empowers her. She enhances her areas of strength or comfort. Finally, this method greatly expands the possibilities of matching products to learning preferences, which should prove more engaging and motivating to the learner.

The more meticulous and intentional you are when selecting products for your list, the better you will address the needs, interests, abilities, and readiness levels of your learners. The more aware you are of what you are offering your students, the better match you can make. Your students also will be more motivated. So, not only do you need to consider the primary learning style that each product embodies, but you also need to consider those secondary styles. With such intention, you will ensure that the product choices you provide are the best possible options for those particular students on specific assignments.

Creating a Product List
Based on Learning Styles

The first step in creating a product list based on learning styles is to determine the learning style platform you will use over the course of a year (or a semester or a unit)—whether that be the one presented here (K, O, T, V, and W plus the concept of *PRIMARYsecondary*) or the ones found in Karnes and Stephens (2000) or VARK (2007). Then you must determine which learning style your students possess through a learning style inventory. Once you decide which products best match your students, it's time to create the Product List for your unit or course. Remember, the more varied you are, the better the learning. Figure 2.1 should be a great start for you.

Now consider the *PRIMARYsecondary* learning style labeling. Remember that the secondary letters can be any combination based on the actual product and its components. Figure 2.2 encourages you to try your hand at this.

How did you do? Figure 2.3 lists the *PRIMARYsecondary* learning style designation. Remember that yours may differ—it all depends upon the actual assignment. For a complete labeling of *PRIMARYsecondary* learning styles for all of the products in Figure 2.1, see Appendix A.

Final Thoughts

When content is more important than product, students' needs, interests, abilities, and readiness levels can be better met with a product list of options for students. These options, however, must be intentionally offered. Not all products are offered every time. If you develop a product list based on learning style and consider the primary and secondary styles inherent in the product, you can ensure differentiation in your instruction. Students don't always have product choices in their comfort zones, so the secondary letters offer the opportunity for them to stretch. The same product list would potentially lead to a student doing the same products over and over. By limiting and changing the list, you encourage exploration and skill development. By requiring authentic products and by authentically assessing those products, you are preparing your students for the 21st century.

Label each product by marking the dominant product type with a capital letter and the other component(s) with lowercase letter(s).

- PowerPoint Presentation _____

- Monologue _____

- Technical Report _____

- Pamphlet _____

- Model _____

- Invention _____

- Essay _____

- Debate _____

- Poster _____

- Graph _____

Figure 2.2. *PRIMARYsecondary* product examples.

Label each product by marking the dominant product type with a capital letter and the other component(s) with lowercase letter(s).

- PowerPoint Presentation <u>Twv</u>

- Monologue <u>Ow or O</u>

- Technical Report <u>W</u>

- Pamphlet <u>Vw</u>

- Model <u>Kv</u>

- Invention <u>Kw or Kwv</u>

- Essay <u>W</u>

- Debate <u>O or Ow or Owk</u>

- Poster <u>Vw</u>

- Graph <u>Vw or Vwt</u>

Figure 2.3. Answer key to *PRIMARYsecondary* product examples.

Chapter 3

The DAP Tool

Components of the DAP Tool

Assessment should be about learning: What does the learner already know about the content? What is he ready to learn? How does he best enjoy learning? What pace is optimal for him to learn the content? What are his learning goals during the unit? How much innovation and creativity has he put into the learning and into showing what he's learned? What did he learn about the content by the end of the unit? What did he learn about himself as a learner by the conclusion of the unit? What is he ready to learn next? This list of questions may be overwhelming, but they are necessary when you focus on student learning.

Unfortunately, too many educators equate assessment with a grade that goes in the grade book. That's only one facet of assessment—that is summative assessment or assessment of learning according to Chappius, Stiggins, Arter, and Chappius (2005). They distinguish between the assessment *of* learning and the assessment *for* learning. Assessment of learning is a summative assessment that comes at the end of a particular learning experience, a proof of learning. They emphasize the importance of formative assessment with ongoing assessment being the key to continuous progress. Chappius and his colleagues called this *assessment for learning*. In part, assessment for learning occurs when "teachers use the classroom assessment process and the continuous flow of information about student achievement that it provides in order to advance, not merely check on, student learning" (Stiggins, 2002, p. 5). Shepard et al. (2005) defined formative assessment as "assessment carried out during the instructional process for the purpose of improving teaching or learning" (p. 275). So, although assessment of learning has a place (usually in the grade book), assessment for learning is what guides learning, placing emphasis on continuous progress.

By assessing products, you can fully answer those last four assessment questions:

1. What did the student learn about the content by the end of the unit?
2. What did he learn about himself as a learner by the end of the unit?
3. How much innovation and creativity has he put into the learning and into showing what's he learned?
4. What is he ready to learn next?

Answers to these questions inform instructional decisions. From the ongoing formative assessment, you gain much information to guide and direct your instruction.

Assessment is indeed multifaceted when considering products. Regardless of the product and regardless of the content, four main components should always be assessed: Content, Presentation, Creativity, and Reflection.

1. *Content* (i.e., what you want the student to learn) is by far the most critical component of any product. After all, the product is simply a vehicle to demonstrate what's learned.
2. The *Presentation* component embodies those characteristics that make the product the specific product; for example, for a pamphlet a learner would manipulate such elements as graphics, text, and design whereas a monologue calls for the integration of script, characterization, voice, and gestures.
3. The *Creativity* component is the individual spark of originality that a creator puts into his creation. That sense of self distinguishes one person's model of an atom from another's model of an atom.
4. Finally, *Reflection* involves the important process of a student analyzing his own learning. Here the student learns the skills of metacognition (thinking about thinking) that will empower him to become a lifelong learner.

So, whether a learner is creating a documentary, mask, or model, these four components will be incorporated and will guide the student when developing products. And, when the educator assesses any product, those same four components will be addressed.

Therefore, every single DAP Tool—regardless of product—will have these four components. So when a student begins to develop the product, the DAP Tool guides her in the development (that's the *D* in DAP) of the product (the *P* part). She will address Content, Presentation, Creativity, and Reflection. Then the educator uses the DAP Tool (here's the *A* part) to assess the product—focusing on those same four components. This one tool, then, serves several purposes. And, because each DAP Tool uses the same components and related vocabulary, the development and assessment of products are simplified. Before you can use the DAP Tool, though, you must explore each component more fully.

Content

Too often educators focus on the product itself instead of the significant content the product is presenting. For example, a state-of-the-art Web page may encompass all of the critical elements of a Web page (the Presentation section of the DAP Tool) in a spectacular, innovative way (the Creativity part) but with very little regard to the content itself. And, if we're not careful, as assessors we may be so impressed with the Web page that we overlook the lack of content or the incorrect content. Regardless of how many bells and whistles a Web page has, if the content is not thoroughly explored (whether it's the structure of a cell or the three branches of government) in an accurate, logical format, then the Web page does not indicate a high level of content attainment. Because the assignment's goal was to learn the significant content and the product was the vehicle to do that, both the learner and the teacher have missed the mark!

So, what exactly are you looking for when you examine content? First of all, the content must be *accurate* and *thorough*. For example, in an essay exploring the causes of the Russian Revolution, the writer must discuss the actual economic, social, and political causes and support them with real, factual detail. He can't argue that Henry the VIII (i.e., wrong ruler of the wrong country) played a critical role or describe how everyone had equal rights under the law (which also is wrong). Likewise, if the learner is writing a speech based on the Bill of Rights, then factual information about the Bill of Rights should be woven throughout the speech. Yes, this seems like a very obvious concept—that content must be accurate—but somehow that obvious concept is ignored in countless classrooms as students receive high grades for splashy products with little content substance.

The second criterion for content is *complexity of thought*: Has the content been thought about in a way that goes beyond a surface understanding? Webb (1999) explored varying Depth of Knowledge (DOK) levels in his studies of assessment alignment:

1. Recall

    Recall of a fact, information, or procedure.

2. Skill/Concept

    Use of information, conceptual knowledge, procedure, two or more steps, etc.

3. Strategic Thinking

    Requires reasoning, developing a plan or sequence of steps; has some complexity; more than one possible answer; generally takes less than 10 minutes to do.

4. Extended Thinking

    Requires an investigation; time to think and process multiple conditions of the problem or task; and more than 10 minutes to do non-routine manipulations. (p. 3)

DOK Levels 1 to 4 go from simple, one-step tasks to very complex tasks with high cognitive demands that may take extended lengths of time. (See Figure 3.1 for Webb's suggested activities for each level.) As educators preparing students for the 21st century, we must focus learning on DOK levels 3 and 4. Too often, we dwell in the first two levels and require students to go no further. Complexity of thought only occurs in the latter levels.

In your education classes, you no doubt studied Bloom's (1956) Taxonomy of Cognitive Objectives. The revised taxonomy (Anderson et al., 2001) was updated by several scholars, including Krathwohl, who worked on the original. To better describe the levels, they changed the nouns to verbs (thus reflecting the active thinking process) and altered the order of the two highest levels so that the levels look like this: remember, understand, apply, analyze, evaluate, and create. Regardless of whether you refer to the original or the new version, the main premise remains the same: All learners must think at high levels. But realize that the process isn't linear. Figure 3.2 shows the interrelationship and interaction of the six cognitive dimensions, plus it emphasizes the critical nature that remembering and understanding the facts have on the possibility of processing those facts at higher levels. The responsibility, then, falls on educators' shoulders to ensure that opportunities for this complexity of thought occur at the upper three levels of the Bloom taxonomy.

Both Bloom and Webb emphasize the varying levels of learning from simple to complex. If students are to be able to compete in a global world,

Depth of Knowledge (DOK) Levels

Figure 3.1. Depth of Knowledge (DOK) levels.

Level One Activities	Level Two Activities	Level Three Activities	Level Four Activities
Recall elements and details of story structure, such as sequence of events, character, plot and setting.	Identify and summarize the major events in a narrative.	Support ideas with details and examples.	Conduct a project that requires specifying a problem, designing and conducting an experiment, analyzing its data, and reporting results/ solutions.
Conduct basic mathematical calculations.	Use context cues to identify the meaning of unfamiliar words.	Use voice appropriate to the purpose and audience.	Apply mathematical model to illuminate a problem or situation.
Label locations on a map.	Solve routine multiple-step problems.	Identify research questions and design investigations for a scientific problem.	
Represent in words or diagrams a scientific concept or relationship.	Describe the cause/effect of a particular event.	Develop a scientific model for a complex situation.	Analyze and synthesize information from multiple sources.
Perform routine procedures like measuring length or using punctuation marks correctly.	Identify patterns in events or behavior.	Determine the author's purpose and describe how it affects the interpretation of a reading selection.	Describe and illustrate how common themes are found across texts from different cultures.
Describe the features of a place or people.	Formulate a routine problem given data and conditions.		Design a mathematical model to inform and solve a practical or abstract situation.
	Organize, represent and interpret data.	Apply a concept in other contexts.	

Note. From *Web Alignment Tool*, by N. L. Webb, 2005, Madison, WI: Wisconsin Center for Educational Research. Retrieved May 27, 2008, from http://www.wcer.wisc.edu/WAT/index.aspx. Reprinted with permission.

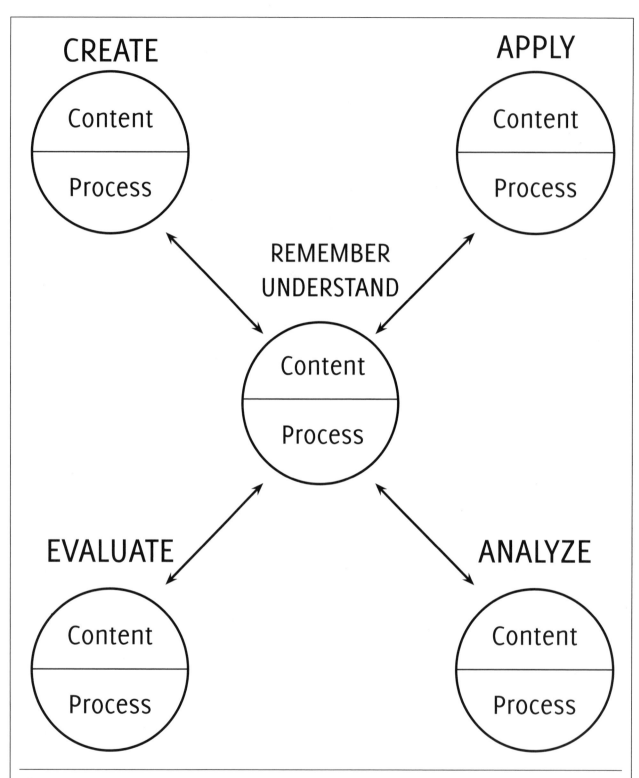

Figure 3.2. The interaction of cognitive dimensions.

Note. From *Strategies for Differentiating Instruction: Best Practices for the Classroom* (p. 69), by J. L. Roberts and T. F. Inman, 2007, Waco, TX: Prufrock Press. Copyright © 2007 by Prufrock Press. Reprinted with permission.

they have to have the complex, cognitive skills needed to do so. They must be sophisticated and original in their thinking and be able to connect to previous learning. So, when the content inherent in a student's product is analyzed, complexity of thought must be considered in addition to the accuracy of the information.

A third criterion for content assessment is *organization*. Is the content presented in a logical, organized way? That organization will differ by content area. It could be structured chronologically, linearly, spatially, or by order of importance, cause and effect, process, classification, comparison and contrast, or problem to solution. Whatever the organization, it should be best suited for both the specific content and the product.

Content, then, is indeed the cornerstone of assessing learning in a product, which is why it is listed first in the DAP Tool. Content must be accurate, complex, and organized. Without those elements, continuous progress proves difficult to determine. Every single DAP Tool, regardless of product, will have the same vocabulary and the same criteria in the Content section.

Presentation

Presentation will be the unique component of the DAP Tool. Whereas Content, Creativity, and Reflection descriptors are uniform across products, descriptors in the Presentation section will be individualized according to the characteristics of the specific product. Here the learner will explore what makes an interview an interview and what distinguishes an essay from a technical report. For example, descriptors for a political cartoon include *purpose*, *text*, *illustration*, and *layout* whereas *purpose*, *construction*, and *specifications* are descriptors for an invention. A pamphlet DAP Tool lists *text*, *graphics*, and *layout* under Presentation, whereas the service-learning project DAP Tool includes *problem solving*, *plan*, and *evidence of making a difference*. Product-specific characteristics or questions must accompany each descriptor to aid the learner in creating the product and the educator in assessing it. Presentation is the component that directs the creation of the product itself—regardless of content. Therefore, a poster will incorporate *text*, *graphics*, and *layout* whether that poster is one describing quadrilaterals, analyzing the fall of Rome, or illustrating the dissection of a starfish.

Creativity

The United States has been the global front-runner in creativity and innovation for a long time. That appears to be changing, however. Kao

(2007) explored this topic in his book *Innovation Nation: How America Is Losing Its Innovation Edge, Why It Matters, and What We Can Do to Get It Back.* In an October 2007 online interview with Amy Bernstein of *strategy+business* magazine, Kao "diagnoses America's ills as a continuing loss of innovation capacity," citing Finland and China as exemplars in innovation: "Beijing recently promulgated its 11th five-year plan, and this one names innovation as the top national priority. . . . They've established very ambitious scientific and technical goals, along with metrics for productivity. They've got a national vision" (p. 1). The Task Force on the Future of American Innovation (2005) concurs:

> For more than half a century, the United States has led the world in scientific discovery and innovation. It has been a beacon, drawing the best scientists to its educational institutions, industries, and laboratories from around the globe. However, in today's rapidly evolving competitive world, the United States can no longer take its supremacy for granted. Nations from Europe to Eastern Asia are on a fast track to pass the United States in scientific excellence and technological innovation. (p. 1)

As Florida (2005) argued in *The Flight of the Creative Class,* "The competition for creative talent is heating up all over the globe" (p. 7). So, what can we do to keep American creativity front and center and encourage innovation? One simple part of that answer lies in teaching and assessing creativity routinely.

Without creativity, there is no innovation. Educators must embed both critical and creative thinking skills into the curriculum. There are models to follow. For example, Torrance (1963) discussed four skills critical to the development of creativity: fluency, flexibility, originality, and elaboration. The Center for Creative Learning (http://www.creativelearning.com) is a wonderful resource for strategies and curricula that address creativity.

An easy way to incorporate creativity is to use the DAP Tool. The third component of the DAP Tool, Creativity encourages the learner to think about the content from varying perspectives and new angles. It guides the learner into developing products that are both unique and original. Creativity, then, is personal insight, that sense of self the learner brings to the content and to the product. Creativity encourages the learner to take ownership through the content's creation. It distinguishes one student's sculpture of a tree from another. By carefully directing the learner to be conscious of creativity in the demonstration of what is learned (i.e., the product), you are encouraging innovation. You are helping to build America's innovation capacity.

Reflection

Reflection, although virtually ignored in most classrooms, may be the most revealing of the four components. Highly personal in nature, reflection involves the learner thinking about her own learning:

- What did I learn about the content by creating this product?
- What did I learn about myself as a learner?
- How did I learn this?
- What's my next step in learning about this content?
- What connections have I made?
- How much effort did I put into the learning?
- How does my effort reflect on the end product?
- How much rigor did the content and product provide?

Each answer proves invaluable for both teacher and student. In fact, Chappius et al. (2005) listed reflection as integral in advancing student learning. They detailed multiple strategies for teachers to embrace including "engaging students in *regular* self-assessment with standards held constant so they can watch themselves grow over time and thus learn to become in charge of their own success" (p. 34). Shepard et al. (2005) argued: "Engaging students in critiquing their own work serves both cognitive and motivational purposes. Ultimately the habit of self-assessment leads to the self-monitoring of performance" (p. 291).

The metacognitive questions encourage a learner to think about how she thinks and empower her to take responsibility for her learning. This thinking serves as impetus for future learning as it encourages young people to be lifelong learners. Savvy teachers will embrace this section of the DAP Tool as the preassessment for future learning—for the differentiation of content, process, and product. If answered thoughtfully and honestly, this reflective piece will afford you the opportunity to analyze both the learner and the learning—and perhaps even the instruction. Examining the student's reflection will enable you to decide the next step to provide in the student's learning.

How do you prepare your students for this reflection to be meaningful? The best approach is to teach them about metacognition and the skills involved. In a paper commissioned by the National Center on Education and Economy for the New Commission on the Skills of the American Workforce, Adams (2006) beautifully blended reflection with creativity (the last two components of the DAP Tool) in her Recommendations for Education. In this paper, *The Sources of Innovation and Creation*, she emphasized the importance of metacognitive skills as she urged educators to "promote the decision to be creative" (p. 50) in addition to promoting an analysis of that creative process:

> . . . educational programs should not only aim to enhance student creativity, but should also directly teach students about the field of creativity itself so that they gain an explicit awareness of their own creative potential, as well as an understanding of methods of enhancement. With this knowledge, they can both make an informed decision to pursue creative activities and at the same time, better control and direct the development of their abilities. This meta-cognition of the creative process should also involve explicit awareness of the practical skills involved in creativity. (p. 50)

She argued, then, that in order for children to be creative, they must know what creativity is and explore and develop those characteristics and skills within themselves. This self-evaluation of learning, this thinking about their thinking, is a skill that follows the students throughout life—while it leads them to meaningful lifelong learning. Metacognition creates the capacity for accepting and acting on feedback from others as well as from one's self.

If a learner actively reflects on her learning for each product she creates, she develops those metacognitive skills that are transferable to any arena. Not only does this high-level thinking serve as impetus for future learning, but it also encourages the learner to take responsibility for making continuous progress in her learning. Each DAP Tool requires reflection; this can be in any format acceptable to both you and your student, whether that be a written piece that accompanies each product or a short discussion between you and the learner. This section of the DAP Tool reveals the actual learning that occurred.

The Tool Itself

Once you understand each component individually (i.e., Content, Presentation, Creativity, and Reflection), you should appreciate the impact this tool as a whole will have on student learning and your approach to instruction. Every single product will be developed and assessed systematically with standard vocabulary and set criteria. Content, the primary focus, will be explored in terms of accuracy, complexity, and organization. Through Presentation, both you and your students will understand and appreciate the unique characteristics that create a specific product. With a focus on Creativity, creative thinking skills will be developed as students learn to express themselves in their learning and in the ways they demonstrate what they've learned. Finally, through Reflection, students will take ownership in their learning as they explore how they think and learn. Neither you nor the learner should be hesitant to explore new products because the DAP Tool will guide you.

The four components are only part of the protocol. The extended Performance Scale coupled with three tiers of increased expectation and sophistication for each product help create a tool that takes the top off learning and allows for easy differentiation of product assessment. Read Chapter 4 to discover how.

Assessment and Differentiation Opportunities With the DAP Tool

You are now familiar with the four components of the DAP Tool: Content, Presentation, Creativity, and Reflection. The next step is to examine both the Performance Scale the DAP Tool uses to assess products and the three tiers of the tool that make it easy for you to differentiate the level of expectation for your students who are ready to raise their sights, perhaps higher than they realized was possible. Both elements of the instrument remove the learning ceiling for students, an essential characteristic for encouraging continuous progress and developing lifelong learners.

The Performance Scale

There is no better way to assess products than to measure performance against standards. Each DAP Tool has the same scale for assessing performance as it relates to standards. Of course, establishing agreed-upon levels of performance is important for you as well as for the student. Everyone needs to know the expectations to reach the different levels of performance. The standard sets the bar, so students and educators alike know how high they must "jump" to reach or exceed the standard. Nothing about the assessment of performance should remain unknown or undecided. Typically state and national curriculum standards dictate the Content component standard. For Presentation, Creativity, and Reflection, you will set the standards. The key to successfully using standards is deciding on the standard that you will accept. Arter and McTighe (2001) stated that "rubrics are not truly complete until we decide on the 'performance standard'—the level of performance on the rubric that we'll call 'meeting standard' or 'being competent'" (p. 73). After setting the standard, you may want to collect examples of products that reach the various performance levels in order to show students the standards you have set. Another way to establish standards is to work with other teachers in your grade or school to establish standards for each level.

The DAP Tool provides a multilevel Performance Scale for you to assess the product in relation to your standards (see Figure 4.1). The Performance Scale actually appears on each DAP Tool to keep the performance standards visible to all, making it easy to keep the focus on expected levels of performance. The seven levels of performance range from 0 to 6.

- The lowest point on the Performance Scale is *nonparticipating*, which equates to zero. This level indicates that nothing was turned in, so the zero is very descriptive of the student's effort (or lack thereof).

- Level 1 is named *nonperforming*. The student did something; however, there was little effort directed toward meeting the standard. Level 1 indicates that the student missed the mark with his product in one or more of the four components: Content, Presentation, Creativity, and Reflection (or in the subcategories of the four components).

- Level 2 is called the *novice* level. Level 2 indicates that the student demonstrated initial awareness and knowledge of the standard. It is a first step toward the standard. Students assessed to be at Level 2 are ready for specific feedback to guide their work toward the standard.

- Level 3 is labeled *progressing*. This name indicates that the student's work demonstrates movement toward the standard. This level is closer to proficiency than the novice level; however, in relationship to the proficient level, the work isn't yet at the standard.

- Level 4 is *proficient*. This is the level expected to meet the standard. This level is the minimum goal expected for all students. Proficient is the mark that state and national standards have set.

- Level 5 is *advanced*. This designation indicates that the student's work has exceeded the standard that has been established. This level is very important for any students who have already met the standard at the proficient level. Without this advanced level, many students will be "running in place" or waiting for other students to reach proficiency. All students need goals that challenge them to make continuous progress.

Meaning of Performance Scale:

6—PROFESSIONAL LEVEL: level expected from a professional in the content area

5—ADVANCED LEVEL: level exceeds expectations of the standard

4—PROFICIENT LEVEL: level expected for meeting the standard

3—PROGRESSING LEVEL: level demonstrates movement toward the standard

2—NOVICE LEVEL: level demonstrates initial awareness and knowledge of standard

1—NONPERFORMING LEVEL: level indicates no effort made to meet standard

0—NONPARTICIPATING LEVEL: level indicates nothing turned in

Figure 4.1. DAP Tool Performance Scale.

Note. Adapted from *Strategies for Differentiating Instruction: Best Practices for the Classroom* (p. 137), by J. L. Roberts and T. F. Inman, 2007, Waco, TX: Prufrock Press. Copyright © 2007 by Prufrock Press. Adapted with permission.

- Level 6 is named *professional*, thus designating the level of performance expected from a professional in a field or in a specific content area. Rarely reached by students, this level provides a target for young people who have the potential to excel at a level well beyond proficiency. Level 6 sets a very high standard for any student, one only occasionally seen in student products. Making the professional level available to young people removes limitations as to what the young person perceives she can accomplish. Level 6 ratchets up the expectations and helps students realize there are levels of achievement beyond distinguished or whatever the highest assessment level is in their state.

This seven-level system (remember, one of the seven levels is zero) establishes a system for assessing each of the four components of the DAP Tool: Content, Presentation, Creativity, and Reflection. The placement of this scale across from each question or description of performance makes it convenient for you to assess performance of each student on each component of each product. What you must have to have clearly in mind is the standard against which the performance is being judged. A sample from the creativity component is in Figure 4.2.

Beyond Proficiency

One innovative and very important aspect of the Performance Scale used with the DAP Tool is that there are two levels of performance above proficient. Proficiency is an admirable goal if your students aren't there yet; however, proficiency is no goal at all for students who are almost at

CONTENT	• Is the content correct and complete?	0 1 2 3 4 5 6
	• Has the content been thought about in a way that goes beyond a surface understanding?	0 1 2 3 4 5 6
	• Is the content put together in such a way that people understand it?	0 1 2 3 4 5 6

Figure 4.2. Tier 1 creativity.

Note. Adapted from *Strategies for Differentiating Instruction: Best Practices for the Classroom,* by J. L. Roberts and T. F. Inman, 2007, Waco, TX: Prufrock Press. Copyright © 2007 by Prufrock Press. Adapted with permission.

proficiency, are at the proficient level, or are beyond the proficient level. Schools must provide opportunities to learn new things every day. School is the place to develop the potential of each student, including the potential of students who have mastered the content at the proficient level. The advanced and professional levels provide incentives for teachers and students to plan and work to exceed the proficient level. In addition, the professional level opens up a new set of possibilities as it establishes standards that are used by professionals in their fields. As a result of realizing that there are levels for products that extend beyond what they have seen in schools, students reconsider self-expectations; and educators, parents, and students rethink societal expectations of performance for young people in K–12 educational settings. For the talented student who can usually throw the assignment together and get a perfect score, the challenge of two levels above proficiency may initially be very uncomfortable. Hopefully, students like that will rise to the challenge when they see both advanced and professional levels that provide targets that require hard work to reach.

The professional level provides a goal that very few students will reach. In a sports context, the professional level for achievement would be Tiger Woods in golf or Wayne Gretsky in hockey. The professional designation raises the level of expectations you have for your students' products, making it clear that adults in their professional lives are responsible for the very products that the students are working on in class. Relevance comes when young people see the professional level as important beyond school. The professional designation sets a performance standard beyond what most students will meet; however, it lets them know that they have a level to which to strive. Some young people aspire to reach the highest levels, but they need guidance and encouragement to do that. The professional level creates real-world importance for high-level products. After all, professionals use products to communicate with target audiences.

PRESENTATION		
REPRESENTATION	▪ Does the sculpture look like what it is? Is it a clear representation?	0 1 2 3 4 5 6
CRAFTSMANSHIP	▪ Is the craftsmanship precise and neat? Was enough time spent on the sculpture?	0 1 2 3 4 5 6

Figure 4.3. Wire sculpture Tier 1 DAP Tool: Presentation.

Note. Used with permission of Paul Johnson, art teacher.

Using the Scale

How do these levels work in a classroom assignment? Let's examine the levels of the Performance Scale that a high school art teacher designated for the wire sculptures he assigned. The Presentation component for the teacher's wire sculpture DAP Tool can be found in Figure 4.3. The two main descriptors are *representation* and *craftsmanship*. Because none of his students had created a wire sculpture before, he only designed a Tier 1 DAP Tool.

Sample sculptures are pictured in Figures 4.4–4.8. Each photograph is followed by a student's comment on the assignment and the instructor's rationale for the assessment.

Performance Level 5

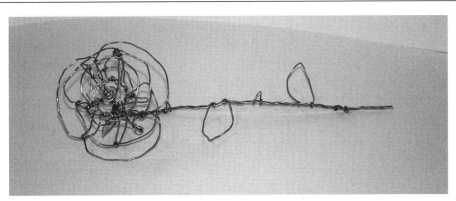

Figure 4.4. Wire sculpture: Advanced.

Note. Used with permission of Paul Johnson, art teacher.

Student Comment: I really enjoyed using wire for this project. I have used wire to make jewelry so I was a little familiar with it. I definitely learned that it was challenging, although I really liked my outcome. Perhaps I will work with wire more in my future.

Teacher Rationale for Performance Level 5: I evaluated this sculpture as a 5 on the DAP Performance Scale. I judged the content to be correct and complete, exceeding the standard of the assignment. The sculpture demonstrated an understanding and awareness that exceeded the standard. The presentation is a clear representation of the subject (a rose). The craftsmanship is precise and neat and exceeds the standard. The student's creativity is apparent as is usage of prior knowledge.

Performance Level 4

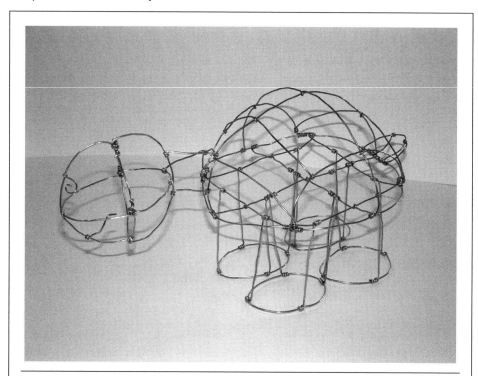

Figure 4.5. Wire sculpture: Proficient.

Note. Used with permission of Paul Johnson, art teacher.

Student Comment: I learned that I could work with wire without stabbing myself a thousand times. I was pleasantly surprised. It wasn't as hard for me as I thought it might be. The only problem I had was getting the legs to all be the same size. It's sometimes hard for me to visualize things in 3-D. It was fun and interesting working with a new material.

Teacher Rationale for Performance Level 4: I evaluated this sculpture as a 4. I judged the content to be correct and complete, meeting the standard for the assignment. The sculpture demonstrates an understanding and awareness of the standard. The presentation is representative of the subject (a turtle). Time and effort were spent on the assignment, and the presentation was neat and skillfully presented. The student displayed creativity and used prior knowledge in a new way.

Performance Level 3

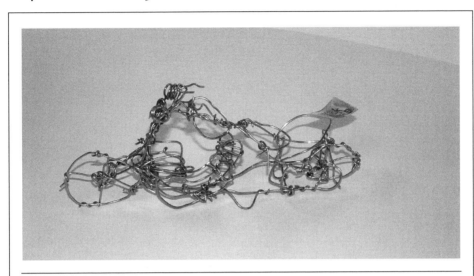

Figure 4.6. Wire sculpture: Progressing.

Note. Used with permission of Paul Johnson, art teacher.

Student Comment: I learned that no matter what you are working with you can't underestimate the difficulty of your project. Although I thought it would be easy, it was really hard working with wire as the wire doesn't cooperate. I learned that I never want to do a wire project again.

Teacher Rationale for Performance Level 3: I evaluated this sculpture as a 3. I judged the content to be mostly correct and complete on the assignment. The sculpture reached a surface understanding and awareness of the standard. The presentation is mostly representative of the subject (a motorcycle). Time and effort were spent on the assignment, but the presentation could have been neater and more skillfully presented. The student displayed some creativity and used prior knowledge in a mostly new way.

Performance Level 2

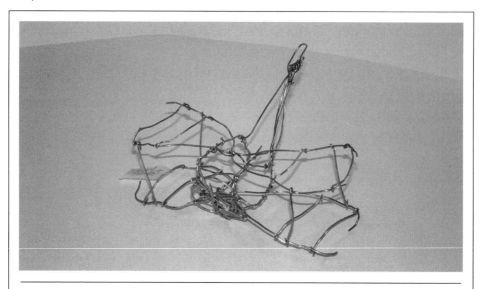

Figure 4.7. Wire sculpture: Novice.

Note. Used with permission of Paul Johnson, art teacher.

Student Comment: I learned that it's harder than it looks. But if you try and use your head, it will be successful. I can do more if I try harder.

Teacher Rationale for Performance Level 2: I evaluated this sculpture as a 2 on the DAP scale. I judged the content to be somewhat correct and complete, but lacking a complete understanding of the assignment. The sculpture reached a surface understanding and awareness of the standard. The presentation is somewhat representative of the subject (a biplane). The presentation could have been better if more time and effort were spent on the assignment. I judged the sculpture to be somewhat creative and representative of applying knowledge in a new way.

Performance Level 1

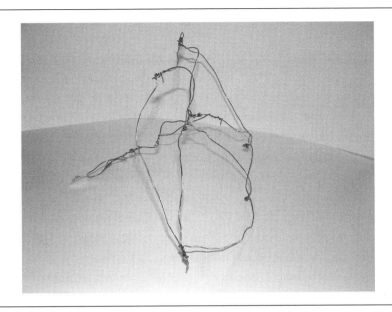

Figure 4.8. Wire sculpture: Nonperforming.

Note. Used with permission of Paul Johnson, art teacher.

Student Comment: I hated this project and hope we don't have to do it again because I didn't know how to bend the wire and get it to stay together. My project is not good, but I couldn't make it any better as it kept falling apart.

Teacher Rationale for Performance Level 1: I evaluated this sculpture as a 1. I judged the content to be both incorrect and incomplete. The sculpture did not reach even a surface understanding and is difficult to identify or understand. The presentation is not a clear representative of the subject (an umbrella). The presentation is haphazard and obviously completed in haste. I judged the sculpture to be uncreative and not representative of applying knowledge in a new way.

Please note that the wire sculpture assignment had no students who received a 0 or a 6. After all, you certainly plan for all students to at least try to complete the assignment, and you don't necessarily expect any to produce the final product at a professional level.

The Three Tiers:
Differentiating and More

Just as the Performance Scale allows for removing the learning ceiling, the three tiers of the DAP Tool for each product provide ready means for you to raise levels of expectation for students who are ready for more advanced work. The three tiers for each DAP Tool are intended to guide students from their initial experience with a specific product (i.e., Tier 1) to versions of the same products that are more advanced (i.e., Tier 2 and Tier 3). For some students, Tier 3 provides a level to which to aspire, knowing what a professional in that area would produce. Of course, some students may begin with the Tier 2 or Tier 3 of the DAP Tool. Prior experiences with the content and the product will determine the appropriate tier.

The DAP Tool at varying tiers allows you to increase the level of expectations for students who are ready to create an increasingly sophisticated product. The DAP Tool, then, provides a ready way to differentiate. For example, all students in your fourth-grade class may be working on an assignment that provides them with the opportunity to show what they have learned about geometry through a PowerPoint presentation. Most of the children have never created a PowerPoint, so they need the Tier 1 DAP Tool on this product. (Remember, your preassessment will guide that instructional decision.) However, in that class there are a few students who have previously worked with PowerPoint. You have the Tier 2 DAP Tool for PowerPoint to give to those students who are beyond the beginning level. Differentiation of expectations is easy when the DAP Tool has been prepared for the three tiers. Tier 3 of the PowerPoint DAP Tool will be there at whatever point the student produces a PowerPoint with such expertise that you think it will be appropriate to introduce the Tier 3 DAP Tool. Then you will introduce a higher level of expectations that raises the bar again.

School grade or age will not determine the appropriate tier of the DAP Tool to use in order to provide a match for specific students. Tiers 1, 2, and 3 for each DAP Tool (whether that be a monologue, podcast, poster, or essay) do not equate to a particular grade in school but rather to a demonstrated performance level in relation to a standard. Ongoing assessment results inform you as to which tier of the DAP Tool is appropriate for which student or cluster of students. Even if you have a homogeneous group of students, at any level, you will find that there will be differing levels of performance; the DAP Tool allows for differentiating instruction via differing tiers for a specific product. You know that the one-size-fits-all approach to expectations dooms some students to frustration either because the expectations are too high or too low. The three different tiers for the DAP

Tool allow you to respond to these differences without writing and rewriting rubrics.

DAP Tools at different tiers make it easy to accommodate the needs, experiences, and interests of all children, including children who are gifted and talented. A child or a cluster of children may be ready for a higher tier of DAP Tool than their peers. The DAP Tool with three tiers ensures that the teacher can provide that challenge. The child who is gifted in creativity will appreciate the role that creativity plays as one of the four components of all DAP Tools. Creativity is expected and, consequently, encouraged. The fact that DAP Tools are developed to appeal to learners who prefer kinesthetic, oral, technological, visual, or written products makes it possible to provide ongoing choices to engage students in learning experiences with a wide variety of products.

One characteristic of effective differentiation strategies is their similarity: Assignments need to look as much alike as possible. The format of the DAP Tool certainly does that. Tier 2 elevates expectations above Tier 1, and Tier 3 does likewise over Tier 2. You will have students with varying levels of experience and expertise with the content and the product; consequently, they will need different expectations to guide them if each is to make continuous progress—and the more similar those expectations appear to the students, the less possibility there will be concerns over "fairness" of assignments. (Actually, they should expect assignments to differ because they understand that they differ from their peers in a myriad of ways!) A very important concept in differentiating assignments is to make the assignment different to address student interests, needs, abilities, or levels of readiness—not to assign more work. The varying tiers of the DAP Tool allow you to provide different expectations for the same assignment. For example, you have assigned the students to conduct a live interview with a veteran of the Korean War. The student who is new to conducting a live interview will need to have the Tier 1 DAP Tool while a student who has successfully conducted interviews will need the Tier 2 Tool, maybe even Tier 3. You never want a student to mark time, but rather want her to be improving skills and learning new content. The varying levels of the DAP Tool have the same format, so they look very similar, making it easy for you to match to the student or cluster of students based on their experience and expertise with the specific assignment. The entire class uses the DAP Tool for live interviews but different tiers guide the development of the product, and selection of the specific tier is intentional, matching the tier to students' expertise and experience.

Let's examine the poster tool to illustrate how expectations change subtly for each of the three tiers with the four components. In the next four

POSTER—DAP TOOL
Content

TIER ONE **CONTENT**	▪ Is the content correct and complete?	0 1 2 3 4 5 6
	▪ Has the content been thought about in a way that goes beyond a surface understanding?	0 1 2 3 4 5 6
	▪ Is the content put together in such a way that people understand it?	0 1 2 3 4 5 6
TIER TWO **CONTENT**	▪ Content is accurate.	0 1 2 3 4 5 6
	▪ Content has depth and complexity of thought.	0 1 2 3 4 5 6
	▪ Content is organized.	0 1 2 3 4 5 6
TIER THREE **CONTENT**	▪ Content is accurate and thorough in detail.	0 1 2 3 4 5 6
	▪ Product shows complex understanding and manipulation of content.	0 1 2 3 4 5 6
	▪ Product shows deep probing of content.	0 1 2 3 4 5 6
	▪ Organization is best suited to the product.	0 1 2 3 4 5 6

Figure 4.9. Poster DAP Tool: Content.

Note. Adapted from *Strategies for Differentiating Instruction: Best Practices for the Classroom* by J. L. Roberts and T. F. Inman, 2007, Waco, TX: Prufrock Press. Copyright © 2007 by Prufrock Press. Adapted with permission.

figures, you will see the three tiers placed together to highlight the purpose and pattern of the tiers. Notice how the language increases in sophistication from tier to tier.

Consider Content first. Figure 4.9 focuses on correctness, organization, and complexity of content. Note that each tier differs in wording and subtly increases the level of expectation.

The second component of the DAP Tool is Presentation. This example of Presentation will show you the progression from Tier 1 to Tier 2 and then to Tier 3 for a poster. For example, note how the graphics go from being important and relevant (Tier 1), to being appropriate and adding information (Tier 2), to enhancing meaning and being best suited (Tier 3). Expectations increase with each tier. Likewise, examine the expectations for text. Tier 1 involves labels explaining graphics, while Tier 2 expects the text to highlight the most important concepts. Tier 3, the most demanding, describes the text as highlighting the most important concepts in a clear, concise manner. Figure 4.10 shows the three tiers for Presentation in detail.

Creativity is the third component. Notice that the levels of sophistication vary from Tier 1 to Tier 2; however, the difference is more dramatic from Tier 1 to Tier 3. (See Figure 4.11.)

Reflection also changes as your students have experience with thinking about what they have learned about the content and about themselves as learners. (See Figure 4.12.) Consider the question "What did you learn about yourself as a learner by creating this product?" (Tier 1) and statements "Reflection on what the student learned about self as a learner is apparent" (Tier 2) and "Insightful reflection on what the student learned about self as a learner is expressed" (Tier 3). Note how they are applicable to different students based on the students' experience, ability, and readiness.

After examining each of the four components for the Poster DAP Tool, consider how the Poster DAP Tool can be used in your classroom in a unit on ecology and conservation. Let's start by asking the question: Is the assignment to design a poster with an environmental message the same for each student in the class? The words in the assignment may be the same; however, the similarities end there because students differ in so many ways. Experiences as well as levels of achievement of the students differ considerably with the environment (the content), designing posters (the product), creativity, and reflection. Consequently, students may need the Poster DAP Tool at Tier 1, Tier 2, or Tier 3 based on your preassessment of their abilities and experiences on all four components of the DAP Tool. Beginners and those with few experiences related to the environment or in designing posters for a purpose will need the Tier 1 Poster DAP Tool (see Figure 4.13). A few students may be ready for Tier 2 (see Figure 4.14). Occasionally, you may have a student ready to start with Tier 3 (see Figure 4.15). The DAP Tool makes differentiated expectations readily available.

POSTER—DAP TOOL
Presentation

TIER ONE PRESENTATION		
TEXT	▪ Is the title easy to see, clear, and well placed? Do the labels clearly explain the graphics?	0 1 2 3 4 5 6
GRAPHICS	▪ Are the graphics (illustrations, photos, etc.) important and relevant to the topic?	0 1 2 3 4 5 6
LAYOUT	▪ Are the images carefully selected and emphasized? Is the labeling linked to the graphic? Is it pleasing to the eye? Is the spacing deliberate to draw attention to main parts of the poster?	0 1 2 3 4 5 6
TIER TWO PRESENTATION		
TEXT	▪ Title enhances the poster's purpose and is well placed. Text highlights most important concepts in topic.	0 1 2 3 4 5 6
GRAPHICS	▪ Graphics (illustrations, photos, etc.) add information and are appropriate for the topic.	0 1 2 3 4 5 6
LAYOUT	▪ Layout design clearly emphasizes graphics in an organized and attractive manner. Text is placed to clearly describe/explain all graphic images. Spacing is carefully planned with consideration of space not used.	0 1 2 3 4 5 6
TIER THREE PRESENTATION		
TEXT	▪ Title, clearly reflecting purpose, is strategically placed. Text highlights most important concepts in clear, concise manner.	0 1 2 3 4 5 6
GRAPHICS	▪ Graphics (illustrations, photos, etc.) enhance meaning and are best suited for the purpose.	0 1 2 3 4 5 6
LAYOUT	▪ Successful composition of graphic images and design concepts communicates the purpose. Text is strategically placed to enhance the message of the poster. Negative space is used to highlight key points.	0 1 2 3 4 5 6

Figure 4.10. Poster DAP Tool: Presentation.

Note. Adapted from *Strategies for Differentiating Instruction: Best Practices for the Classroom*, by J. L. Roberts and T. F. Inman, 2007, Waco, TX: Prufrock Press. Copyright © 2007 by Prufrock Press. Adapted with permission.

POSTER—DAP TOOL
Creativity

TIER ONE CREATIVITY	• Is the content seen in a new way?	0 1 2 3 4 5 6
	• Is the presentation done in a new way?	0 1 2 3 4 5 6
TIER TWO CREATIVITY	• Individual insight is expressed in relation to the content.	0 1 2 3 4 5 6
	• Individual spark is expressed in relation to the presentation.	0 1 2 3 4 5 6
TIER THREE CREATIVITY	• Individual insight is originally expressed in relation to the content.	0 1 2 3 4 5 6
	• Individual spark is originally expressed in relation to the presentation.	0 1 2 3 4 5 6

Figure 4.11. Poster DAP Tool: Creativity.

Note. Adapted from *Strategies for Differentiating Instruction: Best Practices for the Classroom,* by J. L. Roberts and T. F. Inman, 2007, Waco, TX: Prufrock Press. Copyright © 2007 by Prufrock Press. Adapted with permission.

POSTER—DAP TOOL
Reflection

TIER ONE REFLECTION	• What did you learn about the content as you completed this product?	0 1 2 3 4 5 6
	• What did you learn about yourself as a learner by creating this product?	0 1 2 3 4 5 6
TIER TWO REFLECTION	• Reflection on the learning of the content through product development is apparent.	0 1 2 3 4 5 6
	• Reflection on what the student learned about self as a learner is apparent.	0 1 2 3 4 5 6
TIER THREE REFLECTION	• Insightful reflection on the learning of the content through product development is expressed.	0 1 2 3 4 5 6
	• Insightful reflection on what the student learned about self as a learner is expressed.	0 1 2 3 4 5 6

Figure 4.12. Poster DAP Tool: Reflection.

Note. Adapted from *Strategies for Differentiating Instruction: Best Practices for the Classroom,* by J. L. Roberts and T. F. Inman, 2007, Waco, TX: Prufrock Press. Copyright © 2007 by Prufrock Press. Adapted with permission.

POSTER Tier 1—DAP TOOL

CONTENT		
	▪ Is the content correct and complete?	0 1 2 3 4 5 6
	▪ Has the content been thought about in a way that goes beyond a surface understanding?	0 1 2 3 4 5 6
	▪ Is the content put together in such a way that people understand it?	0 1 2 3 4 5 6
PRESENTATION		
TEXT	▪ Is the title easy to see, clear, and well placed? Do the labels clearly explain the graphics?	0 1 2 3 4 5 6
GRAPHICS	▪ Are the graphics (illustrations, photos, etc.) important and relevant to the topic?	0 1 2 3 4 5 6
LAYOUT	▪ Are the images carefully selected and emphasized? Is the labeling linked to the graphic? Is it pleasing to the eye? Is the spacing deliberate to draw attention to main parts of the poster?	0 1 2 3 4 5 6
CREATIVITY	▪ Is the content seen in a new way?	0 1 2 3 4 5 6
	▪ Is the presentation done in a new way?	0 1 2 3 4 5 6
REFLECTION	▪ What did you learn about the content as you completed this product?	0 1 2 3 4 5 6
	▪ What did you learn about yourself as a learner by creating this product?	0 1 2 3 4 5 6

Comments

_____

_____

Meaning of Performance Scale:

6—PROFESSIONAL LEVEL: level expected from a professional in the content area

5—ADVANCED LEVEL: level exceeds expectations of the standard

4—PROFICIENT LEVEL: level expected for meeting the standard

3—PROGRESSING LEVEL: level demonstrates movement toward the standard

2—NOVICE LEVEL: level demonstrates initial awareness and knowledge of standard

1—NONPERFORMING LEVEL: level indicates no effort made to meet standard

0—NONPARTICIPATING LEVEL: level indicates nothing turned in

Figure 4.13. Poster Tier 1.

POSTER Tier 2—DAP TOOL

CONTENT	▪ Content is accurate.	0 1 2 3 4 5 6
	▪ Content has depth and complexity of thought.	0 1 2 3 4 5 6
	▪ Content is organized.	0 1 2 3 4 5 6
PRESENTATION		
TEXT	▪ Title enhances the poster's purpose and is well placed. Text highlights most important concepts in topic.	0 1 2 3 4 5 6
GRAPHICS	▪ Graphics (illustrations, photos, etc.) add information and are appropriate for the topic.	0 1 2 3 4 5 6
LAYOUT	▪ Layout design clearly emphasizes graphics in an organized and attractive manner. Text is placed to clearly describe/explain all graphic images. Spacing is carefully planned with consideration of space not used.	0 1 2 3 4 5 6
CREATIVITY	▪ Individual insight is expressed in relation to the content.	0 1 2 3 4 5 6
	▪ Individual spark is expressed in relation to the presentation.	0 1 2 3 4 5 6
REFLECTION	▪ Reflection on the learning of the content through product development is apparent.	0 1 2 3 4 5 6
	▪ Reflection on what the student learned about self as a learner is apparent.	0 1 2 3 4 5 6

Comments

_____

_____

Meaning of Performance Scale:

6—PROFESSIONAL LEVEL: level expected from a professional in the content area

5—ADVANCED LEVEL: level exceeds expectations of the standard

4—PROFICIENT LEVEL: level expected for meeting the standard

3—PROGRESSING LEVEL: level demonstrates movement toward the standard

2—NOVICE LEVEL: level demonstrates initial awareness and knowledge of standard

1—NONPERFORMING LEVEL: level indicates no effort made to meet standard

0—NONPARTICIPATING LEVEL: level indicates nothing turned in

Figure 4.14. Poster Tier 2.

POSTER Tier 3—DAP TOOL

CONTENT	■ Content is accurate and thorough in detail.	0 1 2 3 4 5 6
	■ Product shows complex understanding and manipulation of content.	0 1 2 3 4 5 6
	■ Product shows deep probing of content.	0 1 2 3 4 5 6
	■ Organization is best suited to the product.	0 1 2 3 4 5 6
PRESENTATION		
TEXT	■ Title, clearly reflecting purpose, is strategically placed. Text highlights most important concepts in clear, concise manner.	0 1 2 3 4 5 6
GRAPHICS	■ Graphics (illustrations, photos, etc.) enhance meaning and are best suited for the purpose.	0 1 2 3 4 5 6
LAYOUT	■ Successful composition of graphic images and design concepts communicates the purpose. Text is strategically placed to enhance the message of the poster. Negative space is used to highlight key points.	0 1 2 3 4 5 6
CREATIVITY	■ Individual insight is originally expressed in relation to the content.	0 1 2 3 4 5 6
	■ Individual spark is originally expressed in relation to the presentation.	0 1 2 3 4 5 6
REFLECTION	■ Insightful reflection on the learning of the content through product development is expressed.	0 1 2 3 4 5 6
	■ Insightful reflection on what the student learned about self as a learner is expressed.	0 1 2 3 4 5 6

Comments

Meaning of Performance Scale:
6—PROFESSIONAL LEVEL: level expected from a professional in the content area
5—ADVANCED LEVEL: level exceeds expectations of the standard
4—PROFICIENT LEVEL: level expected for meeting the standard
3—PROGRESSING LEVEL: level demonstrates movement toward the standard
2—NOVICE LEVEL: level demonstrates initial awareness and knowledge of standard
1—NONPERFORMING LEVEL: level indicates no effort made to meet standard
0—NONPARTICIPATING LEVEL: level indicates nothing turned in

Figure 4.15. Poster Tier 3.

Point Total	Percentage Grade
66	100%
55–65	95%
44–54	90%
38–43	80%
33–37	75%
27–32	70%
22–26	65%
below 22 not accepted	

Figure 4.16. Sample grading table.

Grading

This discussion would be incomplete without addressing the important topic of grading. Arter and McTighe (2001) described grading as "the classroom parallel to setting performance standards" (p. 73). They discussed two ways to use rubrics to grade: holistic and analytical approaches. "A *holistic* rubric gives a single score or rating for an entire product or performance based on an overall impression of a student's work" (p. 18). They went on to say, "An *analytical trait* rubric divides a product or performance into essential traits or dimensions so that they can be judged separately— one *analyzes* a product or performance for essential *traits*" (p. 18). With the DAP Tool, the essential traits are the four components. Most of the time, you will choose to use the DAP Tool in the analytical manner. You will want to provide feedback on the components of the DAP Tool on the specific assignment. But, some of the time, you will use the holistic approach as was illustrated in the example of the wire sculpture earlier in this chapter.

Tallying points on the DAP Tool isn't necessarily the answer, but you may choose to use points to establish the grade on the assignment. You can establish a scale to do this. One teacher presents a way to use points on a DAP Tool as a grade. She took the total number of descriptors (11 on the particular DAP Tool she was using). She equated full points for Level 4 proficient on the Performance Scale. She made the 11 scores equivalent and set up the following table in Figure 4.16 to assign grades.

A total point approach probably isn't the best approach because different DAP Tools would have varying total points depending on the product—there are more or fewer points on the Presentation component. You could always weight one aspect over another depending on your instructional goals. For example, you could choose to put emphasis on voice in an essay and, consequently, would want to double or triple points that demonstrate the student's use of voice in the assignment. You are the one who will establish how you assign a grade for a student's work on a product. You will have to decide if using points to establish the grade works best for you on a particular assignment or if a more holistic approach would work best.

Realistically, in addition to feedback, you often will need to provide a letter grade. You will assign a weight to the grade based on your assessment of the importance of the product in your grading period. For example, your students are completing a project as the culminating activity in your unit. Obviously, that project will have a weight much greater than the learning experiences that were a part of the unit. You may have a unit that is teaching the students how to produce a product—for example, a movie or a diary. Once again, the weight will be considered according to the importance of the product to the goals of your unit. You will determine that weight. Remember that, as the instructional leader, you must match assignment to child and grades to assignments. This careful matching of content, process, product, and assessment to child allows you to reach the overall goal of continuous progress for each student.

Final Thoughts

In order to promote continuous progress in your students, maintaining high expectations is a must, especially in a differentiated classroom (Roberts & Inman, 2007). In fact, "these expectations must be two-fold: One, teachers must have high expectations for their students, and, two, students must have high expectations for themselves" (Roberts & Inman, 2007, p. 21). A scale that removes the learning ceiling (i.e., the seven-level Performance Scale of the DAP Tool) encourages high expectations for both you and your students. The professional level especially embodies this concept. Students understand that this same scale will dictate expectations for all products they create. The consistency in expectations coupled with the consistency of the four components and the descriptors provides a strong assessment foundation. Students know they will be held to high standards and will work to meet those expectations.

Because students differ according to abilities, interests, and readiness levels, your expectations for them will differ as well. Once you have preassessed, you can choose which of the three tiers is most appropriate for each student depending on the content, process, and product. Tier 1 is for someone new to the product or the content. Tier 2 matches those with experience, and Tier 3 is appropriate for those ready for a challenge. Differentiation is simplified. The DAP Tool encourages both high expectations and differentiation.

Read on to the next chapter to learn about additional ways to use the DAP Tool to make your class engaging to students.

Chapter 5

Using the DAP Tool

Now that you understand the benefits of a product protocol—especially the consistent vocabulary and uniformity of design for any product—you are ready to explore the uses of the DAP Tool. The four components ensure consistency, the Performance Scale takes the ceiling off the learning, and the three tiers for each product encourage meaningful differentiation. All together, these elements create a tool that changes the way learners create products and the way you assess those products.

Implementation

In the smallest capacity, a DAP Tool can be used as a one-time tool. Suppose that a product is absolutely critical to the learning in a unit or that the entire unit culminates in the creation of this product. The DAP Tool could be used to introduce the learner to the product, guide the development of the product, and supply the means for assessing the product. The DAP Tool, then, provides the guidance for students as to your expectations for the product (especially as far as the presentation is concerned). For example, a middle school social studies class is learning to write a Document-Based Question (DBQ). The DBQ DAP Tool could serve as the guiding force for the unit. You can fully discuss content in a DBQ and what constitutes accuracy, organization, and complexity. You would elaborate on what the DBQ is as you explore the presentation component. Your discussion would include phrasing such as *supporting evidence*, *primary and secondary sources*, *argument*, and *historical analysis*. Then you'd focus on creativity and how important personal insight and interpretation are to the content and to the product. Finally, you would detail the reflection piece as you encourage students to explore their own learning as far as the DBQ is concerned. The natural product for this unit is the DBQ itself. The DAP Tool, used this one time, has served as the content to be learned throughout the unit, a tool to guide the student in writing a DBQ, and ultimately your guide in assessing that DBQ.

Another way to incorporate DAP Tools into student learning is to broaden the use. A classroom could use DAP Tools to establish a protocol for developing and assessing products to utilize throughout the school year. Imagine the pluses! After initial introduction to the tool, the students have specific guidance for any product they create. They may be much more willing to try new products or to venture from their learning style comfort zone with a DAP Tool leading their way. You and your students now share a common vocabulary (Content, Presentation, Creativity, and Reflection) that eases discussion and expectations for all products. The Performance Scale for each product is the same—again, simplifying expectations. When you have to explain a new rubric that looks for different elements each time you give product choices, you waste valuable learning time. Likewise, if the performance scales change with those products, not only is learning time lost during the explanation, but the opportunity for confusion arises as students try to distinguish one scale from another and the reasoning behind them. You may very well use only one tier of the DAP Tool, particularly if the product is new to everyone or if students are new to the idea of Creativity or Reflection being assessed. The three tiers easily allow for differentiation so that you are better matching the needs, interests, abilities, and readiness levels of your students to the content, process, and product. Differentiation also can occur with product choice. Think how easily a student can go to the file cabinet or computer and locate the appropriate DAP Tool for a different product! You can be much more flexible in product options. Winebrenner (2001) argued that students should always have choices in products unless the product is the content (e.g., students are learning how to conduct an experiment in science class). Now, when a student comes to you asking to do a podcast instead of a pamphlet to show you what he's learned about the cell, you can easily say, "Sure!" You won't even consider the time necessary to create a new scoring guide or the expertise needed to know what to put on the rubric. You can simply send him to the DAP Tool warehouse in your room. In short, adoption of the DAP Tool in a classroom provides more time for learning, ease in differentiation, guidance for the learner, encouragement for exploration, and simplification of assessment.

Now imagine an entire school that adopts the DAP Tool. Gone are the arguments: "But Mrs. So-and-so didn't teach it that way last year" or "That's not what Mr. Whatsit expected." Take the benefits described earlier and multiply it by the number of classrooms in your school. Imagine the ease! Think about the consistency in expectations, product development, and assessment. Consider the time that could be spent on new learning and continuous progress when the time spent on discussion of new products, explanation of individual teacher expectations and grading scales, and development of brand-new rubrics (much less on multiple levels) is greatly reduced. Yes, you will still need to teach students how to make products if they've never created them before. However, if the teacher down the hall in a different discipline used that product last year with those same students, erase that from your lesson plan. You only will be responsible for those products never attempted or for the student who transferred in last year. Of course, the school's staff would need to agree on what the standard is for the products, and ideally you would collect product examples to show students. Consider how powerful a school bank of model products would be. Also, consider the implications of an entire school differentiating for their students. Again, imagine the pluses!

Now incorporate the tool on an even larger scale so that an entire school district or system utilizes the DAP Tool. The benefits are exponential! All of the ideas discussed previously from differentiation to consistent expectations now transfer from building to building instead of just classroom to classroom or unit to unit. As students move from one school to another, their transition is eased as they enter a school with the same protocol for developing and assessing products. Learning is uninterrupted. As students transition from elementary to middle school or middle to high school, the protocol remains the same. Expectations for sophistication will differ in products as students progress from Tier 1 to Tier 2 or even Tier 3, but everything else remains the same. Imagine what could be done with the weeks lost by teaching varying expectations and new rubrics for each product assigned by each teacher at each grade level and subject at each school in the entire district! DAP Tools just make sense.

Differentiating With DAP Tools

Differentiation occurs when three specific questions are asked and answered:

1. *Planning Question*—What do I want students to know, understand, and be able to do?

2. *Preassessing Question*—Who already knows, understands, and/or can use the content or demonstrate the skill?
3. *Differentiation Question*—What can I do for him, her, or them so they can make continuous progress and extend their learning? (Roberts & Inman, 2007, pp. 8–9)

The DAP Tool plays a role in all three questions. If the product is the content (e.g., a technology class is creating movies), then the DAP Tool can help present the content. Although this isn't the main use of DAP Tools, the Planning Question is addressed. A more frequent use of the tool answers the Preassessing Question. Each component of the DAP Tool serves as an individual preassessment. For example, if the Content section indicated mostly below-standard assessments for accuracy, organization, or complexity, then moving on with content should be done with caution. Likewise, if the learner had great difficulty on the Presentation component, before he creates that product again, direct teaching about the product would need to occur. Little attention to Creativity indicates that creative thinking skills should be taught. Finally, and perhaps most telling, is the Reflection section. Here the learner honestly and objectively considers her learning. So, if she indicates that very little was learned during the process, then perhaps more (or less) challenging material is warranted. Similarly, if the product proved too simple, then greater complexity (perhaps increasing the tier) is needed. Analysis of a learner's metacognition is a powerful preassessment. Content, process, and product all can be assessed with the same tool.

The third question also can be addressed by the DAP Tool through differentiation of assessment. The DAP Tool allows ease in differentiating assessment while maintaining high standards. This systematic and equitable protocol encourages you to challenge each child based on your preassessment. For example, one learner who is advanced in science or who has a strong understanding of the concept you're teaching in your third-grade science class may be working on a Tier 2 Experiment DAP Tool while the rest use Tier 1. All are being held accountable for the same components just by varying levels of sophistication. The preassessment may indicate that a Tier 1 is needed for a child exposed to the content or the product for the first time. The varying tiers allow you to have high expectations for all children in your class and encourage the children to have high expectations for themselves. After all, maintaining high expectations is one of the principles of a differentiated classroom (Roberts & Inman, 2007).

Oftentimes these high standards prove most challenging for young people who are gifted and talented. In fact, Sanders (1998), the founder of the Value-Added Research and Assessment Center, explained that students with the highest ability are less likely than their peers to make a one-year achievement gain in one year! All children deserve to make continuous progress, including those of high ability. Student growth is related to teacher expectations. Without appropriate expectations for each student, underachievement could be imminent and continuous progress will be blocked.

In addition to varying levels of expectations through the tiers of the DAP Tool, another way to use the tool when differentiating is to encourage individual choice. Students can choose which product to create to demonstrate their learning. Most will lean toward their primary or dominant learning style (the capital letter in the learning style designation; see Chapter 2). Others will take the secondary lower case learning styles into consideration. Thanks to the ease of the DAP Tool, students could choose something not on the list and use a premade DAP Tool for development and assessment.

You also could purposely assign products for individual students or clusters of students. For example, your preassessment indicates that several students have already mastered the unit. Winebrenner (2001) argued that, if a student has 80% or greater proficiency, then he is ready to move on. Let him do that by matching the DAP Tool to the individual student's level of readiness. The same works for a cluster of students who have indicated mastery on a preassessment. Differentiation is all about discovering ways to meet learners' interests, needs, and abilities. Differentiation of content, process, product, and assessment all are possible by implementing the DAP Tool.

Preparing Students for the 21st Century

The first decade of the 21st century tells us that we as a country are facing a great challenge. Fishman's (2006) *China, Inc: How the Rise of the Next Superpower Challenges America* and Friedman's (2007) *The World Is Flat 3.0* explain how China and India are excelling technologically, economically, and academically. Early in the century, the United States Commission on National Security/21st Century (2001) said in its report, *Road Map for National Security: Imperative for Change*:

Second only to a weapon of mass destruction detonating in an American city, we can think of nothing more dangerous than a failure to manage properly science, technology, and education for the common good over the next quarter century. . . . The capacity of America's educational system to create a 21st century workforce second to none in the world is a national security issue of the first order. As things stand, this country is forfeiting that capacity. (pp. 30, 38)

The need for innovation and rigor in our schools is very real, indeed, and the need must be met if we are to thrive.

The Partnership for 21st Century Skills (2007) explained what type of education is needed in order to prepare our students for the changing world:

> While today's schools show the influence of industrial and information age models, the 21st century modern school must appropriately employ both individualized and large scale approaches to assessment. It must bring together rigorous content and real world relevance. It must focus on cognitive skills as well as those in affective and aesthetic domains. It must be attentive to the needs of the individual child and to society as a whole. (p. 6)

Although a tall order, the 21st Century Learning Skills outlined by the Partnership fit the bill. The Partnership (2007) further highlights three learning and innovation skills that "facilitate the mastery of the other 21st century skills" (p. 11): critical thinking and problem solving, creativity and innovation, and communication and collaboration. In addition, information, media, and technology skills, plus life and career skills are described. Many of these skills, from problem solving to initiative and self-direction, are evident in the DAP Tool. The DAP Tool actively engages the learner throughout the learning process, encouraging thought and skill development each step of the way.

The DAP Tool, through its four components and unique approach, is definitely a 21st-century teaching and learning tool, one to use to prepare students for 21st-century challenges. Content, the first component of the DAP Tool, explores accuracy, complexity, and organization. Critical thinking and problem solving are encouraged as the learner analyzes the pertinence of the information, delves deeply into the content to make complex connections, and logically organizes the information. The DAP Tool encourages high-level thinking that incorporates skills from the upper levels of Bloom's taxonomy and DOK Levels 3 and 4 (see Chapter 3). In addition to critical thinking and problem solving, the content component also develops skills in information literacy through the access, evaluation, and use of information. Of course, different forms of media would be explored in the acquisition of content, so media literacy skills also are developed.

The second component, Presentation, analyzes those characteristics inherent in the product itself, and therefore can develop multiple skills depending on the product. Of course, critical thinking and problem solving come into play as the product is created. Information communication and technology (ICT) literacy also are strengthened depending on the product. All products that incorporate technology (from podcasts, to videos, to pamphlets) develop ICT literacy.

Creativity, the third component, is synonymous with the second learning and innovation skill: creativity and innovation. Rarely do educators purposefully develop creative thinking skills in a structured way. Through consistent use of the DAP Tool, creativity and the teaching of creative thinking would be integral parts of any product ever created in class. Learners would begin to think about their creativity in a metacognitive way as they deliberately focus on this component in the development of their products. So, instead of creativity sharply declining at fourth grade (Torrance, 1963), perhaps we'd see a steady growth of creativity throughout the school years. The encouragement and expectations of the learner's creativity and capacity for innovation would transfer from the school environment to the working world.

The last component, Reflection, calls for the learner to analyze his own learning of content and self in the process of creating the product. This metacognition greatly reflects life and career skills. When students reflect on their learning, they analyze their flexibility and adaptability, their initiative and self-direction, their productivity and accountability, and their leadership and responsibility. This self-analysis encourages growth as they dissect what they learned, how they learned it, why they learned it, and what role they as learners took in making that learning happen. Hopefully, reflection will become a habit. All tie directly to 21st-century skills (Partnership, 2007):

> As the research has shown, when students exercise self-control, when they are able to defer short-term gratification for the long-term gain, when they empathize with and are helpful to others, and when they take responsibility for their actions—they are able to function at a higher level. And when this effect is multiplied across the classroom, the rising tide lifts us all. (p. 22)

The DAP Tool, then, when adopted classroom-wide—or even school- or district-wide—would help create that type of learner.

Other innovative aspects of the DAP Tool also develop 21st-century skills. The Performance Scale that removes the ceiling on learning especially addresses the life and career skills. It illustrates to learners that proficiency may not be good enough in a competitive global market. Students are invited to challenge themselves, to discover areas for improvement, and to do just that. The Partnership for 21st Century Skills (2007) explained: "In our global technological age, young people . . . need to demonstrate leadership and take responsibility for results, show initiative and resourcefulness, and be productive and accountable for their actions" (p. 21). The seven-level Performance Scale encourages such skills. Finally, the three tiers of assessment for each product tie in beautifully to 21st-century skills. When each student is held accountable for working at a challenging level just beyond his comfort zone (i.e., Vygotsky's [1978] zone of proximal development), greater learning occurs. As discussed earlier, in order to develop skills relative to their needs and readiness, learners must be preassessed and have learning matched to their interests, needs, readiness levels, and abilities. The DAP Tool, from promoting differentiation to developing problem-solving skills, plays a strong role in developing 21st-century skills in today's learners.

Final Thoughts

DAP Tools, then, can be used for a single assignment or multiple assignments, by one teacher, one school, or an entire district. They can be used to differentiate instruction through preassessment and differentiate assessment through their multiple tiers. DAP Tools also help prepare young people to compete in the 21st-century world. By encouraging the use of varied products to demonstrate what the student has learned, DAP Tools engage children, motivate students, have real-world connections, require high-level thinking and problem-solving skills, accommodate learning preferences, allow for self-expression and creativity, promote ownership and pride in one's work, and develop lifelong learners. Plus, their consistency of language and expectations simplifies the whole process! This protocol can make profound differences in your teaching and in your students' learning. Now, to get started, all you need are the DAP Tools. You'll find plenty in Chapter 6.

DAP Tools, DAP Tools, and More DAP Tools

By this time, you realize the important role products can play in a differentiated classroom, school, or school system—especially when trying to challenge your students. You also know that an ideal way to approach products is through learning style or preference, particularly the *PRIMARYsecondary* avenue. You now understand the philosophy behind the DAP Tool and have intimate knowledge of its components. You recognize the value of the Performance Scale that takes the ceiling off learning and the three tiers of assessment that simplify differentiation. In short, you've been introduced to a new protocol for developing and assessing products. Now, you're ready to use it.

What follows are many samples of DAP Tools. Arranged by their primary learning style (i.e., Kinesthetic, Oral, Technological, Visual, and Written), the examples are many. Products that are primarily kinesthetic are as follows: diorama, experiment, invention, mask, model, sculpture, and service-learning project. DAP tools for oral products include debate, interview (interviewer and interviewee), interview (recorded), monologue, oral report/presentation, and speech (oral). Examples of DAP Tools for technological products are computer graphic, computer program, documentary, movie, podcast, PowerPoint, and Web page. DAP Tools developed for the visual learners include cartoon, collage, graph, pamphlet, pie chart, political cartoon, and poster. Written products that can be assessed with DAP Tools include document-based question, diary, essay, interview (written), letter (business and friendly), speech (written), and technical report. You will find Tiers 1, 2, and 3 for each example. Enjoy!

DIORAMA Tier 1—DAP TOOL

CONTENT	• Is the content correct and complete?	0 1 2 3 4 5 6
	• Has the content been thought about in a way that goes beyond a surface understanding?	0 1 2 3 4 5 6
	• Is the content put together in such a way that people understand it?	0 1 2 3 4 5 6
PRESENTATION		
REPRESENTATION	• Does the diorama look like what it represents? Is it a clear representation? Does it have detail?	0 1 2 3 4 5 6
CONSTRUCTION	• Is the diorama sturdy? Are all sides of the inner area used? Are the items in the diorama balanced?	0 1 2 3 4 5 6
LABELS	• Are the labels clear?	0 1 2 3 4 5 6
EXPLANATION	• Is there a clear explanation of how items in the diorama relate to the assignment?	0 1 2 3 4 5 6
CREATIVITY	• Is the content seen in a new way?	0 1 2 3 4 5 6
	• Is the presentation done in a new way?	0 1 2 3 4 5 6
REFLECTION	• What did you learn about the content as you completed this product?	0 1 2 3 4 5 6
	• What did you learn about yourself as a learner by creating this product?	0 1 2 3 4 5 6

Comments

_____

_____

Meaning of Performance Scale:

6—PROFESSIONAL LEVEL: level expected from a professional in the content area

5—ADVANCED LEVEL: level exceeds expectations of the standard

4—PROFICIENT LEVEL: level expected for meeting the standard

3—PROGRESSING LEVEL: level demonstrates movement toward the standard

2—NOVICE LEVEL: level demonstrates initial awareness and knowledge of standard

1—NONPERFORMING LEVEL: level indicates no effort made to meet standard

0—NONPARTICIPATING LEVEL: level indicates nothing turned in

DIORAMA Tier 2—DAP TOOL

CONTENT	• Content is accurate.	0 1 2 3 4 5 6
	• Content has depth and complexity of thought	0 1 2 3 4 5 6
	• Content is organized.	0 1 2 3 4 5 6
PRESENTATION		
REPRESENTATION	• The diorama makes the viewers see the purpose clearly (whether realistically or symbolically).	0 1 2 3 4 5 6
CONSTRUCTION	• The diorama is built to scale. It is constructed with detail. Materials/media enhance its meaning. The 3-D representation is balanced and proportional.	0 1 2 3 4 5 6
LABELS	• Labels are clear and pertinent.	0 1 2 3 4 5 6
EXPLANATION	• A written or oral explanation fully explains how the representation and construction of the diorama address the assignment.	0 1 2 3 4 5 6
CREATIVITY	• Individual insight is expressed in relation to the content.	0 1 2 3 4 5 6
	• Individual spark is expressed in relation to the presentation.	0 1 2 3 4 5 6
REFLECTION	• Reflection on the learning of the content through product development is apparent.	0 1 2 3 4 5 6
	• Reflection on what the student learned about self as a learner is apparent.	0 1 2 3 4 5 6

Comments

_____

_____

Meaning of Performance Scale:

6—PROFESSIONAL LEVEL: level expected from a professional in the content area

5—ADVANCED LEVEL: level exceeds expectations of the standard

4—PROFICIENT LEVEL: level expected for meeting the standard

3—PROGRESSING LEVEL: level demonstrates movement toward the standard

2—NOVICE LEVEL: level demonstrates initial awareness and knowledge of standard

1—NONPERFORMING LEVEL: level indicates no effort made to meet standard

0—NONPARTICIPATING LEVEL: level indicates nothing turned in

DIORAMA Tier 3—DAP TOOL

CONTENT	▪ Content is accurate and thorough in detail.	0 1 2 3 4 5 6
	▪ Product shows complex understanding and manipulation of content.	0 1 2 3 4 5 6
	▪ Product shows deep probing of content.	0 1 2 3 4 5 6
	▪ Organization is best suited to the product.	
PRESENTATION		
REPRESENTATION	▪ The diorama employs a new idea in the representation.	0 1 2 3 4 5 6
CONSTRUCTION	▪ The construction as to detail, materials, and use of the space is unique to highlight the diorama's purpose.	0 1 2 3 4 5 6
LABELS	▪ Labels effectively direct the purpose of the diorama.	0 1 2 3 4 5 6
EXPLANATION	▪ A written or oral explanation insightfully explains how the representation and construction of the diorama uniquely address the assignment.	0 1 2 3 4 5 6
CREATIVITY	▪ Individual insight is originally expressed in relation to the content.	0 1 2 3 4 5 6
	▪ Individual spark is originally expressed in relation to the presentation.	0 1 2 3 4 5 6
REFLECTION	▪ Insightful reflection on the learning of the content through product development is expressed.	0 1 2 3 4 5 6
	▪ Insightful reflection on what the student learned about self as a learner is expressed.	0 1 2 3 4 5 6

Comments

Meaning of Performance Scale:

6—PROFESSIONAL LEVEL: level expected from a professional in the content area

5—ADVANCED LEVEL: level exceeds expectations of the standard

4—PROFICIENT LEVEL: level expected for meeting the standard

3—PROGRESSING LEVEL: level demonstrates movement toward the standard

2—NOVICE LEVEL: level demonstrates initial awareness and knowledge of standard

1—NONPERFORMING LEVEL: level indicates no effort made to meet standard

0—NONPARTICIPATING LEVEL: level indicates nothing turned in

EXPERIMENT Tier 1—DAP TOOL

CONTENT	▪ Is the content correct and complete?	0 1 2 3 4 5 6
	▪ Has the content been thought about in a way that goes beyond a surface understanding?	0 1 2 3 4 5 6
	▪ Is the content put together in such a way that people understand it?	0 1 2 3 4 5 6
PRESENTATION		
RESEARCH QUESTION AND HYPOTHESIS	▪ Is there a research question in the form of a sentence that explains what was studied? Does the hypothesis explain the outcome that will most likely happen? Does it answer the research question?	0 1 2 3 4 5 6
VARIABLES	▪ Did you describe what you changed (the independent variable)? Did you explain what changed because of the independent variable (the dependent variable)? Did you describe what things remained constant (the controlled variables)? Did you explain how you controlled variables?	0 1 2 3 4 5 6
PROCEDURE	▪ Did you explain your step-by-step process? Are instructions included so that someone could do the same experiment based on this information? Are instructions in logical order, labeled, and numbered? Are instructions in complete sentences? What assumptions have you made?	0 1 2 3 4 5 6
OBSERVATION/DATA COLLECTION	▪ Have you presented all of the data collected during the experiment in an organized way? Are the charts and graphs titled and labeled with units?	0 1 2 3 4 5 6
RESULTS/ CONCLUSIONS/ INFERENCES	▪ Did you tell what happened in the experiment using correct vocabulary? Did you explain if the data supported or did not support the hypothesis? What assumptions can be drawn from the experiment? How does the experiment relate to real life? What changes would you make if you repeated the experiment?	0 1 2 3 4 5 6
CREATIVITY	▪ Is the content seen in a new way?	0 1 2 3 4 5 6
	▪ Is the presentation done in a new way?	0 1 2 3 4 5 6
REFLECTION	▪ What did you learn about the content as you completed this product?	0 1 2 3 4 5 6
	▪ What did you learn about yourself as a learner by creating this product?	0 1 2 3 4 5 6

Comments

_____

_____

Meaning of Performance Scale:

6—PROFESSIONAL LEVEL: level expected from a professional in the content area

5—ADVANCED LEVEL: level exceeds expectations of the standard

4—PROFICIENT LEVEL: level expected for meeting the standard

3—PROGRESSING LEVEL: level demonstrates movement toward the standard

2—NOVICE LEVEL: level demonstrates initial awareness and knowledge of standard

1—NONPERFORMING LEVEL: level indicates no effort made to meet standard

0—NONPARTICIPATING LEVEL: level indicates nothing turned in

EXPERIMENT Tier 2—DAP TOOL

CONTENT	▪ Content is accurate.	0 1 2 3 4 5 6
	▪ Content has depth and complexity of thought.	0 1 2 3 4 5 6
	▪ Content is organized.	0 1 2 3 4 5 6
PRESENTATION		
RESEARCH QUESTION AND HYPOTHESIS	▪ The research question clearly explains what was studied. It provides enough detail to warrant an investigation. The hypothesis clearly explains the probable outcome and identifies variables.	0 1 2 3 4 5 6
VARIABLES	▪ The independent, dependent, and controlled variables are fully explained in detail. The methods for controlling the variables are explained.	0 1 2 3 4 5 6
PROCEDURE	▪ The design and step-by-step process are so clearly explained that a replication of the experiment is possible. The explanation is logical, correct in format, and detailed as to equipment, measurement, and process.	0 1 2 3 4 5 6
OBSERVATION/DATA COLLECTION	▪ Charts and graphs clearly and accurately present all data gleaned from the experiment including multi-trials. Charts and graphs illustrate significant trends, patterns, and results.	0 1 2 3 4 5 6
RESULTS/ CONCLUSIONS/ INFERENCES	▪ Using scientific vocabulary, the results of the experiment are clearly and accurately discussed. The results are fully explained identifying sources of error and citing data as evidence. Conclusions are drawn, inferences are made, and real-world connections are discussed.	0 1 2 3 4 5 6
CREATIVITY	▪ Individual insight is expressed in relation to the content.	0 1 2 3 4 5 6
	▪ Individual spark is expressed in relation to the presentation.	0 1 2 3 4 5 6
REFLECTION	▪ Reflection on the learning of the content through product development is apparent.	0 1 2 3 4 5 6
	▪ Reflection on what the student learned about self as a learner is apparent.	0 1 2 3 4 5 6

Comments

_____

_____

Meaning of Performance Scale:

6—PROFESSIONAL LEVEL: level expected from a professional in the content area

5—ADVANCED LEVEL: level exceeds expectations of the standard

4—PROFICIENT LEVEL: level expected for meeting the standard

3—PROGRESSING LEVEL: level demonstrates movement toward the standard

2—NOVICE LEVEL: level demonstrates initial awareness and knowledge of standard

1—NONPERFORMING LEVEL: level indicates no effort made to meet standard

0—NONPARTICIPATING LEVEL: level indicates nothing turned in

EXPERIMENT Tier 3—DAP TOOL

CONTENT	▪ Content is accurate and thorough in detail.	0 1 2 3 4 5 6
	▪ Product shows complex understanding and manipulation of content.	0 1 2 3 4 5 6
	▪ Product shows deep probing of content.	0 1 2 3 4 5 6
	▪ Organization is best suited to the product.	0 1 2 3 4 5 6
PRESENTATION		
RESEARCH QUESTION AND HYPOTHESIS	▪ The research question accurately explains what will be studied and provides ample detail to warrant an investigation. The well-worded hypothesis clearly explains the probable outcome and accurately identifies variables. Context is provided.	0 1 2 3 4 5 6
VARIABLES	▪ The independent, dependent, and controlled variables are skillfully explained. Methods for controlling variables are described. Assumptions concerning which variables should be controlled are discussed.	0 1 2 3 4 5 6
PROCEDURE	▪ The design and step-by-step process is so richly explained that a replication of the experiment is easily done. The clear explanation is logical, precise in format, and extremely detailed as to equipment, measurement, and process.	0 1 2 3 4 5 6
OBSERVATION/DATA COLLECTION	▪ Well-labeled, clear charts and graphs skillfully and accurately present all data gleaned from the experiment including multi-trials. Charts and graphs support trends, patterns, and results.	0 1 2 3 4 5 6
RESULTS/ CONCLUSIONS/ INFERENCES	▪ Using scientific vocabulary, the results of the experiment are skillfully and accurately analyzed. The results are explained in detail identifying sources of error and citing data as evidence. Insightful conclusions are drawn, and inferences as to scientific implications and real-world connections are fully discussed.	0 1 2 3 4 5 6
CREATIVITY	▪ Individual insight is originally expressed in relation to the content.	0 1 2 3 4 5 6
	▪ Individual spark is originally expressed in relation to the presentation.	0 1 2 3 4 5 6
REFLECTION	▪ Insightful reflection on the learning of the content through product development is expressed.	0 1 2 3 4 5 6
	▪ Insightful reflection on what the student learned about self as a learner is expressed.	0 1 2 3 4 5 6

Comments

_____

_____

Meaning of Performance Scale:

6—PROFESSIONAL LEVEL: level expected from a professional in the content area

5—ADVANCED LEVEL: level exceeds expectations of the standard

4—PROFICIENT LEVEL: level expected for meeting the standard

3—PROGRESSING LEVEL: level demonstrates movement toward the standard

2—NOVICE LEVEL: level demonstrates initial awareness and knowledge of standard

1—NONPERFORMING LEVEL: level indicates no effort made to meet standard

0—NONPARTICIPATING LEVEL: level indicates nothing turned in

INVENTION Tier 1—DAP TOOL

CONTENT	▪ Is the content correct and complete?	0 1 2 3 4 5 6
	▪ Has the content been thought about in a way that goes beyond a surface understanding?	0 1 2 3 4 5 6
	▪ Is the content put together in such a way that people understand it?	0 1 2 3 4 5 6
PRESENTATION		
PURPOSE	▪ Does the invention address a need or solve a problem? Is it a new or improved approach to a problem? Is it useful?	0 1 2 3 4 5 6
CONSTRUCTION	▪ Is the invention stable? Are the materials appropriate for the invention? Will it survive repeated operation?	0 1 2 3 4 5 6
SPECIFICATIONS	▪ Does the invention have written material with it that explains what it is and its use? Are there drawings or descriptions that help in understanding its purpose and how it works? Could someone use it based on the specifications?	0 1 2 3 4 5 6
CREATIVITY	▪ Is the content seen in a new way?	0 1 2 3 4 5 6
	▪ Is the presentation done in a new way?	0 1 2 3 4 5 6
REFLECTION	▪ What did you learn about the content as you completed this product?	0 1 2 3 4 5 6
	▪ What did you learn about yourself as a learner by creating this product?	0 1 2 3 4 5 6

Comments

_____

_____

Meaning of Performance Scale:

6—PROFESSIONAL LEVEL: level expected from a professional in the content area

5—ADVANCED LEVEL: level exceeds expectations of the standard

4—PROFICIENT LEVEL: level expected for meeting the standard

3—PROGRESSING LEVEL: level demonstrates movement toward the standard

2—NOVICE LEVEL: level demonstrates initial awareness and knowledge of standard

1—NONPERFORMING LEVEL: level indicates no effort made to meet standard

0—NONPARTICIPATING LEVEL: level indicates nothing turned in

INVENTION Tier 2—DAP TOOL

CONTENT	▪ Content is accurate.	0 1 2 3 4 5 6
	▪ Content has depth and complexity of thought.	0 1 2 3 4 5 6
	▪ Content is organized.	0 1 2 3 4 5 6
PRESENTATION		
PURPOSE	▪ The invention clearly solves a real problem and/or addresses a specific need in a practical, new approach. It is both useful and unique.	0 1 2 3 4 5 6
CONSTRUCTION	▪ The invention is constructed with detail and shows economy of materials and construction. Materials enhance the purpose of the invention.	0 1 2 3 4 5 6
SPECIFICATIONS	▪ The written specifications describe the invention fully detailing its use and purpose. It includes drawings, descriptions, charts, and so forth that explain how it works. Others should be able to use and understand the invention based on the specifications.	0 1 2 3 4 5 6
CREATIVITY	▪ Individual insight is expressed in relation to the content.	0 1 2 3 4 5 6
	▪ Individual spark is expressed in relation to the presentation.	0 1 2 3 4 5 6
REFLECTION	▪ Reflection on the learning of the content through product development is apparent.	0 1 2 3 4 5 6
	▪ Reflection on what the student learned about self as a learner is apparent.	0 1 2 3 4 5 6

Comments

_____

_____

Meaning of Performance Scale:

6—PROFESSIONAL LEVEL: level expected from a professional in the content area

5—ADVANCED LEVEL: level exceeds expectations of the standard

4—PROFICIENT LEVEL: level expected for meeting the standard

3—PROGRESSING LEVEL: level demonstrates movement toward the standard

2—NOVICE LEVEL: level demonstrates initial awareness and knowledge of standard

1—NONPERFORMING LEVEL: level indicates no effort made to meet standard

0—NONPARTICIPATING LEVEL: level indicates nothing turned in

INVENTION Tier 3—DAP TOOL

CONTENT		
	▪ Content is accurate and thorough in detail.	0 1 2 3 4 5 6
	▪ Product shows complex understanding and manipulation of content.	0 1 2 3 4 5 6
	▪ Product shows deep probing of content	0 1 2 3 4 5 6
	▪ Organization is best suited to the product.	0 1 2 3 4 5 6
PRESENTATION		
PURPOSE	▪ The invention cleverly solves a rather challenging problem and/or addresses an authentic need in an effective way. It is novel in both idea and construction. It is useful and operates in the way it was intended; no other invention addresses the need in exactly the same way. It is nonobvious in that it is sufficiently different from what has been used before.	0 1 2 3 4 5 6
CONSTRUCTION	▪ The construction as to detail and materials is unique to support the purpose of the invention. The invention shows elegance of design and construction.	0 1 2 3 4 5 6
SPECIFICATIONS	▪ Specifications clearly and concisely explain the purpose, function, and use of the invention. Graphics and text purposely reveal its essence. Someone could utilize the invention based on the specifications.	0 1 2 3 4 5 6
CREATIVITY	▪ Individual insight is originally expressed in relation to the content.	0 1 2 3 4 5 6
	▪ Individual spark is originally expressed in relation to the presentation.	0 1 2 3 4 5 6
REFLECTION	▪ Insightful reflection on the learning of the content through product development is expressed.	0 1 2 3 4 5 6
	▪ Insightful reflection on what the student learned about self as a learner is expressed.	0 1 2 3 4 5 6

Comments

_____

_____

Meaning of Performance Scale:

6—PROFESSIONAL LEVEL: level expected from a professional in the content area

5—ADVANCED LEVEL: level exceeds expectations of the standard

4—PROFICIENT LEVEL: level expected for meeting the standard

3—PROGRESSING LEVEL: level demonstrates movement toward the standard

2—NOVICE LEVEL: level demonstrates initial awareness and knowledge of standard

1—NONPERFORMING LEVEL: level indicates no effort made to meet standard

0—NONPARTICIPATING LEVEL: level indicates nothing turned in

MASK Tier 1—DAP TOOL

CONTENT		
	▪ Is the content correct and complete?	0 1 2 3 4 5 6
	▪ Has the content been thought about in a way that goes beyond a surface understanding?	0 1 2 3 4 5 6
	▪ Is the content put together in such a way that people understand it?	0 1 2 3 4 5 6
PRESENTATION		
CONCEPT	▪ Is the mask a realistic or symbolic representation? Does it bring about emotions, thoughts, or moods in the viewer? Is the purpose of the mask evident?	0 1 2 3 4 5 6
CRAFTSMANSHIP	▪ Is the choice of materials appropriate? Has thoughtful attention been paid to detail?	0 1 2 3 4 5 6
ELEMENTS AND PRINCIPLES OF DESIGN	▪ Have some design elements been considered and incorporated such as 3-D form, line, shape, color, texture, and space? Have some design principles been considered and incorporated such as balance and symmetry, unity, or proportion?	0 1 2 3 4 5 6
CREATIVITY	▪ Is the content seen in a new way?	0 1 2 3 4 5 6
	▪ Is the presentation done in a new way?	0 1 2 3 4 5 6
REFLECTION	▪ What did you learn about the content as you completed this product?	0 1 2 3 4 5 6
	▪ What did you learn about yourself as a learner by creating this product?	0 1 2 3 4 5 6

Comments

_____

_____

Meaning of Performance Scale:

6—PROFESSIONAL LEVEL: level expected from a professional in the content area

5—ADVANCED LEVEL: level exceeds expectations of the standard

4—PROFICIENT LEVEL: level expected for meeting the standard

3—PROGRESSING LEVEL: level demonstrates movement toward the standard

2—NOVICE LEVEL: level demonstrates initial awareness and knowledge of standard

1—NONPERFORMING LEVEL: level indicates no effort made to meet standard

0—NONPARTICIPATING LEVEL: level indicates nothing turned in

MASK Tier 2—DAP TOOL

CONTENT	• Content is accurate.	0 1 2 3 4 5 6
	• Content has depth and complexity of thought.	0 1 2 3 4 5 6
	• Content is organized.	0 1 2 3 4 5 6
PRESENTATION		
CONCEPT	• The mask is purposefully realistic or symbolic in its representation. It evokes emotions, moods, and/or thoughts. The viewers see the purpose clearly.	0 1 2 3 4 5 6
CRAFTSMANSHIP	• Materials/media are appropriate and enhance its purpose and meaning. Attention to detail has been carefully considered and executed. The 3-D representation is balanced and proportional. Planning is evident.	0 1 2 3 4 5 6
ELEMENTS AND PRINCIPLES OF DESIGN	• Design elements (i.e., form, line, space, color, shape, and texture) have been carefully considered and integrated. Design principles (especially balance, unity, and proportion) have been successfully integrated.	0 1 2 3 4 5 6
CREATIVITY	• Individual insight is expressed in relation to the content.	0 1 2 3 4 5 6
	• Individual spark is expressed in relation to the presentation.	0 1 2 3 4 5 6
REFLECTION	• Reflection on the learning of the content through product development is apparent.	0 1 2 3 4 5 6
	• Reflection on what the student learned about self as a learner is apparent.	0 1 2 3 4 5 6

Comments

_____

_____

Meaning of Performance Scale:

6—PROFESSIONAL LEVEL: level expected from a professional in the content area

5—ADVANCED LEVEL: level exceeds expectations of the standard

4—PROFICIENT LEVEL: level expected for meeting the standard

3—PROGRESSING LEVEL: level demonstrates movement toward the standard

2—NOVICE LEVEL: level demonstrates initial awareness and knowledge of standard

1—NONPERFORMING LEVEL: level indicates no effort made to meet standard

0—NONPARTICIPATING LEVEL: level indicates nothing turned in

MASK Tier 3—DAP TOOL

CONTENT	• Content is accurate and thorough in detail.	0 1 2 3 4 5 6
	• Product shows complex understanding and manipulation of content.	0 1 2 3 4 5 6
	• Product shows deep probing of content.	0 1 2 3 4 5 6
	• Organization is best suited to the product.	0 1 2 3 4 5 6
PRESENTATION		
CONCEPT	• The mask employs a new idea in the representation, whether that representation is symbolic or realistic. This is evident to the viewer as he experiences emotions, thoughts, and feelings when viewing it. Its purpose is enhanced through representation and materials.	0 1 2 3 4 5 6
CRAFTSMANSHIP	• The craftsmanship as to detail, materials, construction, and media is unique to highlight the mask's purpose. Careful planning has guided the success.	0 1 2 3 4 5 6
ELEMENTS AND PRINCIPLES OF DESIGN	• Design elements (i.e., form, line, space, color, shape, and texture) have been artistically and thoughtfully manipulated. Design principles (especially balance, unity, and proportion) also have been artistically and thoughtfully manipulated.	0 1 2 3 4 5 6
CREATIVITY	• Individual insight is originally expressed in relation to the content.	0 1 2 3 4 5 6
	• Individual spark is originally expressed in relation to the presentation.	0 1 2 3 4 5 6
REFLECTION	• Insightful reflection on the learning of the content through product development is expressed.	0 1 2 3 4 5 6
	• Insightful reflection on what the student learned about self as a learner is expressed.	0 1 2 3 4 5 6

Comments

_____

_____

Meaning of Performance Scale:

6—PROFESSIONAL LEVEL: level expected from a professional in the content area

5—ADVANCED LEVEL: level exceeds expectations of the standard

4—PROFICIENT LEVEL: level expected for meeting the standard

3—PROGRESSING LEVEL: level demonstrates movement toward the standard

2—NOVICE LEVEL: level demonstrates initial awareness and knowledge of standard

1—NONPERFORMING LEVEL: level indicates no effort made to meet standard

0—NONPARTICIPATING LEVEL: level indicates nothing turned in

MODEL Tier 1—DAP TOOL

CONTENT	▪ Is the content correct and complete?	0 1 2 3 4 5 6
	▪ Has the content been thought about in a way that goes beyond a surface understanding?	0 1 2 3 4 5 6
	▪ Is the content put together in such a way that people understand it?	0 1 2 3 4 5 6
PRESENTATION		
REPRESENTATION	▪ Does the model look like what it represents? Is it a clear representation?	0 1 2 3 4 5 6
CONSTRUCTION	▪ Does the construction make the model stable? Are the materials appropriate for the construction?	0 1 2 3 4 5 6
LABELS	▪ Are the labels clear?	0 1 2 3 4 5 6
CREATIVITY	▪ Is the content seen in a new way?	0 1 2 3 4 5 6
	▪ Is the presentation done in a new way?	0 1 2 3 4 5 6
REFLECTION	▪ What did you learn about the content as you completed this product?	0 1 2 3 4 5 6
	▪ What did you learn about yourself as a learner by creating this product?	0 1 2 3 4 5 6

Comments

_____

_____

Meaning of Performance Scale:

6—PROFESSIONAL LEVEL: level expected from a professional in the content area

5—ADVANCED LEVEL: level exceeds expectations of the standard

4—PROFICIENT LEVEL: level expected for meeting the standard

3—PROGRESSING LEVEL: level demonstrates movement toward the standard

2—NOVICE LEVEL: level demonstrates initial awareness and knowledge of standard

1—NONPERFORMING LEVEL: level indicates no effort made to meet standard

0—NONPARTICIPATING LEVEL: level indicates nothing turned in

Note. Adapted from *Strategies for Differentiating Instruction: Best Practices for the Classroom* (p. 208), by J. L. Roberts and T. F. Inman, 2007, Waco, TX: Prufrock Press. Copyright © 2007 by Prufrock Press. Adapted with permission.

MODEL Tier 2—DAP TOOL

CONTENT	▪ Content is accurate.	0 1 2 3 4 5 6
	▪ Content has depth and complexity of thought.	0 1 2 3 4 5 6
	▪ Content is organized.	0 1 2 3 4 5 6
PRESENTATION		
REPRESENTATION	▪ The model makes the viewers see the purpose (whether realistically or symbolically).	0 1 2 3 4 5 6
CONSTRUCTION	▪ The model is built to scale. The model is constructed with detail. Materials enhance the meaning of the model.	0 1 2 3 4 5 6
LABELS	▪ Labels are clear and match the key.	0 1 2 3 4 5 6
CREATIVITY	▪ Individual insight is expressed in relation to the content.	0 1 2 3 4 5 6
	▪ Individual spark is expressed in relation to the presentation.	0 1 2 3 4 5 6
REFLECTION	▪ Reflection on the learning of the content through product development is apparent.	0 1 2 3 4 5 6
	▪ Reflection on what the student learned about self as a learner is apparent.	0 1 2 3 4 5 6

Comments

Meaning of Performance Scale:
6—PROFESSIONAL LEVEL: level expected from a professional in the content area
5—ADVANCED LEVEL: level exceeds expectations of the standard
4—PROFICIENT LEVEL: level expected for meeting the standard
3—PROGRESSING LEVEL: level demonstrates movement toward the standard
2—NOVICE LEVEL: level demonstrates initial awareness and knowledge of standard
1—NONPERFORMING LEVEL: level indicates no effort made to meet standard
0—NONPARTICIPATING LEVEL: level indicates nothing turned in

Note. Adapted from *Strategies for Differentiating Instruction: Best Practices for the Classroom* (p. 209), by J. L. Roberts and T. F. Inman, 2007, Waco, TX: Prufrock Press. Copyright © 2007 by Prufrock Press. Adapted with permission.

MODEL Tier 3—DAP TOOL

CONTENT	▪ Content is accurate and thorough in detail.	0 1 2 3 4 5 6
	▪ Product shows complex understanding and manipulation of content.	0 1 2 3 4 5 6
	▪ Product shows deep probing of content.	0 1 2 3 4 5 6
	▪ Organization is best suited to the product.	0 1 2 3 4 5 6
PRESENTATION		
REPRESENTATION	▪ The model employs a new idea in the representation.	0 1 2 3 4 5 6
CONSTRUCTION	▪ The construction as to the detail and materials is unique to highlight the model's purpose.	0 1 2 3 4 5 6
LABELS	▪ Labels direct the purpose of the model.	0 1 2 3 4 5 6
CREATIVITY	▪ Individual insight is originally expressed in relation to the content.	0 1 2 3 4 5 6
	▪ Individual spark is originally expressed in relation to the presentation.	0 1 2 3 4 5 6
REFLECTION	▪ Insightful reflection on the learning of the content through product development is expressed.	0 1 2 3 4 5 6
	▪ Insightful reflection on what the student learned about self as a learner is expressed.	0 1 2 3 4 5 6

Comments

_____

_____

Meaning of Performance Scale:

6—PROFESSIONAL LEVEL: level expected from a professional in the content area

5—ADVANCED LEVEL: level exceeds expectations of the standard

4—PROFICIENT LEVEL: level expected for meeting the standard

3—PROGRESSING LEVEL: level demonstrates movement toward the standard

2—NOVICE LEVEL: level demonstrates initial awareness and knowledge of standard

1—NONPERFORMING LEVEL: level indicates no effort made to meet standard

0—NONPARTICIPATING LEVEL: level indicates nothing turned in

Note. Adapted from *Strategies for Differentiating Instruction: Best Practices for the Classroom* (p. 210), by J. L. Roberts and T. F. Inman, 2007, Waco, TX: Prufrock Press. Copyright © 2007 by Prufrock Press. Adapted with permission.

SCULPTURE Tier 1—DAP TOOL

CONTENT	• Is the content correct and complete?	0 1 2 3 4 5 6
	• Has the content been thought about in a way that goes beyond a surface understanding?	0 1 2 3 4 5 6
	• Is the content put together in such a way that people understand it?	0 1 2 3 4 5 6
PRESENTATION		
CONCEPT	• Is the sculpture a realistic or symbolic representation? Does it bring about emotions or thoughts in the viewer? Is the title appropriate to the content and form?	0 1 2 3 4 5 6
CRAFTSMANSHIP	• Is it sturdy? Are appropriate materials used for construction? Is attention to detail paid successfully?	0 1 2 3 4 5 6
ELEMENTS AND PRINCIPLES OF DESIGN	• Have some design elements been considered and incorporated such as form, space, color, shape, or texture? Have some design principles been applied and incorporated such as balance, movement, unity, or harmony? Does the sculpture keep viewers interested and encourage them to walk around it?	0 1 2 3 4 5 6
CREATIVITY	• Is the content seen in a new way?	0 1 2 3 4 5 6
	• Is the presentation done in a new way?	0 1 2 3 4 5 6
REFLECTION	• What did you learn about the content as you completed this product?	0 1 2 3 4 5 6
	• What did you learn about yourself as a learner by creating this product?	0 1 2 3 4 5 6

Comments

_____

_____

Meaning of Performance Scale:

6—PROFESSIONAL LEVEL: level expected from a professional in the content area

5—ADVANCED LEVEL: level exceeds expectations of the standard

4—PROFICIENT LEVEL: level expected for meeting the standard

3—PROGRESSING LEVEL: level demonstrates movement toward the standard

2—NOVICE LEVEL: level demonstrates initial awareness and knowledge of standard

1—NONPERFORMING LEVEL: level indicates no effort made to meet standard

0—NONPARTICIPATING LEVEL: level indicates nothing turned in

SCULPTURE Tier 2—DAP TOOL

CONTENT	▪ Content is accurate.	0 1 2 3 4 5 6
	▪ Content has depth and complexity of thought.	0 1 2 3 4 5 6
	▪ Content is organized.	0 1 2 3 4 5 6
PRESENTATION		
CONCEPT	▪ The sculpture is purposefully realistic or symbolic in its representation. It evokes emotions, moods, or thoughts. The viewer sees the purpose clearly. Title reflects sculptural concept and form.	0 1 2 3 4 5 6
CRAFTSMANSHIP	▪ The choice of materials/media enhances the meaning. Attention to detail has been paid. The 3-D representation is balanced and proportional. Planning is evident.	0 1 2 3 4 5 6
ELEMENTS AND PRINCIPLES OF DESIGN	▪ Design elements (i.e., form, space, color, shape, and texture) have been carefully considered and integrated. Design principles (especially balance, movement, unity, and harmony) have been effectively integrated. The viewer is compelled to walk around the sculpture as it strongly captures his attention and interest.	0 1 2 3 4 5 6
CREATIVITY	▪ Individual insight is expressed in relation to the content.	0 1 2 3 4 5 6
	▪ Individual spark is expressed in relation to the presentation.	0 1 2 3 4 5 6
REFLECTION	▪ Reflection on the learning of the content through product development is apparent.	0 1 2 3 4 5 6
	▪ Reflection on what the student learned about self as a learner is apparent.	0 1 2 3 4 5 6

Comments

_____

_____

Meaning of Performance Scale:

6—PROFESSIONAL LEVEL: level expected from a professional in the content area

5—ADVANCED LEVEL: level exceeds expectations of the standard

4—PROFICIENT LEVEL: level expected for meeting the standard

3—PROGRESSING LEVEL: level demonstrates movement toward the standard

2—NOVICE LEVEL: level demonstrates initial awareness and knowledge of standard

1—NONPERFORMING LEVEL: level indicates no effort made to meet standard

0—NONPARTICIPATING LEVEL: level indicates nothing turned in

SCULPTURE Tier 3—DAP TOOL

CONTENT	• Content is accurate and thorough in detail.	0 1 2 3 4 5 6
	• Product shows complex understanding and manipulation of content.	0 1 2 3 4 5 6
	• Product shows deep probing of content.	0 1 2 3 4 5 6
	• Organization is best suited to the product.	0 1 2 3 4 5 6
PRESENTATION		
CONCEPT	• The sculpture employs a new idea in the representation, whether that representation is symbolic or realistic. This is evident to the viewer as he experiences emotions, thoughts, and feelings when viewing it. Title enhances the concept.	0 1 2 3 4 5 6
CRAFTSMANSHIP	• The craftsmanship as to detail, materials, construction, and media is unique to highlight the sculpture's purpose. Careful planning is evident.	0 1 2 3 4 5 6
ELEMENTS AND PRINCIPLES OF DESIGN	• Design elements (i.e., form, space, color, shape, and texture) have been artistically and thoughtfully manipulated. Design principles (especially balance, movement, unity, and harmony) also have been artistically and thoughtfully manipulated. The viewer becomes one with the sculpture.	0 1 2 3 4 5 6
CREATIVITY	• Individual insight is originally expressed in relation to the content.	0 1 2 3 4 5 6
	• Individual spark is originally expressed in relation to the presentation.	0 1 2 3 4 5 6
REFLECTION	• Insightful reflection on the learning of the content through product development is expressed.	0 1 2 3 4 5 6
	• Insightful reflection on what the student learned about self as a learner is expressed.	0 1 2 3 4 5 6

Comments

_____

_____

Meaning of Performance Scale:

6—PROFESSIONAL LEVEL: level expected from a professional in the content area

5—ADVANCED LEVEL: level exceeds expectations of the standard

4—PROFICIENT LEVEL: level expected for meeting the standard

3—PROGRESSING LEVEL: level demonstrates movement toward the standard

2—NOVICE LEVEL: level demonstrates initial awareness and knowledge of standard

1—NONPERFORMING LEVEL: level indicates no effort made to meet standard

0—NONPARTICIPATING LEVEL: level indicates nothing turned in

SERVICE-LEARNING PROJECT Tier 1—DAP TOOL

CONTENT	▪ Is the content correct and complete?	0 1 2 3 4 5 6
	▪ Has the content been thought about in a way that goes beyond a surface understanding?	0 1 2 3 4 5 6
	▪ Is the content put together in such a way that people understand it?	0 1 2 3 4 5 6
PRESENTATION		
PROBLEM SOLVING	▪ Is there a problem to be solved? Is the problem real and important? Does the community or group believe it is a problem? Does the community need or want help in solving it?	0 1 2 3 4 5 6
PLAN	▪ Has a step-by-step plan been worked out to solve the problem? Have responsibilities been assigned? Has a timeline been established? Are resources identified and used? Is the plan implemented in a friendly, efficient way?	0 1 2 3 4 5 6
EVIDENCE OF MAKING A DIFFERENCE	▪ Has the project reached the desired results? Are more steps needed? Has the community or group benefitted? How can that be proven? What evidence is there that the goals were reached?	0 1 2 3 4 5 6
CREATIVITY	▪ Is the content seen in a new way?	0 1 2 3 4 5 6
	▪ Is the presentation done in a new way?	0 1 2 3 4 5 6
REFLECTION	▪ What did you learn about the content as you completed this product?	0 1 2 3 4 5 6
	▪ What did you learn about yourself as a learner by creating this product?	0 1 2 3 4 5 6

Comments

Meaning of Performance Scale:

6—PROFESSIONAL LEVEL: level expected from a professional in the content area

5—ADVANCED LEVEL: level exceeds expectations of the standard

4—PROFICIENT LEVEL: level expected for meeting the standard

3—PROGRESSING LEVEL: level demonstrates movement toward the standard

2—NOVICE LEVEL: level demonstrates initial awareness and knowledge of standard

1—NONPERFORMING LEVEL: level indicates no effort made to meet standard

0—NONPARTICIPATING LEVEL: level indicates nothing turned in

SERVICE-LEARNING PROJECT Tier 2—DAP TOOL

CONTENT	▪ Content is accurate.	0 1 2 3 4 5 6
	▪ Content has depth and complexity of thought.	0 1 2 3 4 5 6
	▪ Content is organized.	0 1 2 3 4 5 6
PRESENTATION		
PROBLEM SOLVING	▪ The identified problem is apparent in the real world and needs addressing. The community agrees that the problem needs addressing and that help is needed to make it happen.	0 1 2 3 4 5 6
PLAN	▪ A plan has been worked out with goals, responsibilities, and a timeline. Resources are identified and used. Plan is implemented in a respectful and efficient way.	0 1 2 3 4 5 6
EVIDENCE OF MAKING A DIFFERENCE	▪ Results of the service project have been analyzed, and the problem has been addressed in a satisfactory way. The community agrees. If not, next steps are planned.	0 1 2 3 4 5 6
CREATIVITY	▪ Individual insight is expressed in relation to the content.	0 1 2 3 4 5 6
	▪ Individual spark is expressed in relation to the presentation.	0 1 2 3 4 5 6
REFLECTION	▪ Reflection on the learning of the content through product development is apparent.	0 1 2 3 4 5 6
	▪ Reflection on what the student learned about self as a learner is apparent.	0 1 2 3 4 5 6

Comments

_____

_____

Meaning of Performance Scale:

6—PROFESSIONAL LEVEL: level expected from a professional in the content area

5—ADVANCED LEVEL: level exceeds expectations of the standard

4—PROFICIENT LEVEL: level expected for meeting the standard

3—PROGRESSING LEVEL: level demonstrates movement toward the standard

2—NOVICE LEVEL: level demonstrates initial awareness and knowledge of standard

1—NONPERFORMING LEVEL: level indicates no effort made to meet standard

0—NONPARTICIPATING LEVEL: level indicates nothing turned in

SERVICE-LEARNING PROJECT Tier 3—DAP TOOL

CONTENT	▪ Content is accurate and thorough in detail.	0 1 2 3 4 5 6
	▪ Product shows complex understanding and manipulation of content.	0 1 2 3 4 5 6
	▪ Product shows deep probing of content.	0 1 2 3 4 5 6
	▪ Organization is best suited to the product.	
PRESENTATION		
PROBLEM SOLVING	▪ Problem identified merits intervention. Community or a group acknowledges the necessity of intervention to address the problem.	0 1 2 3 4 5 6
PLAN	▪ Appropriate, reachable goals are expressed in measurable terms. Resources are utilized to fullest extent. All strategies relate directly to meeting goals. Plan is implemented in an efficient, courteous manner.	0 1 2 3 4 5 6
EVIDENCE OF MAKING A DIFFERENCE	▪ Analysis of data provides evidence of the effectiveness of the service project in solving the problem. Plans are made to complete or continue the project.	0 1 2 3 4 5 6
CREATIVITY	▪ Individual insight is originally expressed in relation to the content.	0 1 2 3 4 5 6
	▪ Individual spark is originally expressed in relation to the presentation.	0 1 2 3 4 5 6
REFLECTION	▪ Insightful reflection on the learning of the content through product development is expressed.	0 1 2 3 4 5 6
	▪ Insightful reflection on what the student learned about self as a learner is expressed.	0 1 2 3 4 5 6

Comments

_____

_____

Meaning of Performance Scale:

6—PROFESSIONAL LEVEL: level expected from a professional in the content area

5—ADVANCED LEVEL: level exceeds expectations of the standard

4—PROFICIENT LEVEL: level expected for meeting the standard

3—PROGRESSING LEVEL: level demonstrates movement toward the standard

2—NOVICE LEVEL: level demonstrates initial awareness and knowledge of standard

1—NONPERFORMING LEVEL: level indicates no effort made to meet standard

0—NONPARTICIPATING LEVEL: level indicates nothing turned in

DEBATE Tier 1—DAP TOOL

CONTENT	• Is the content correct and complete?	0 1 2 3 4 5 6
	• Has the content been thought about in a way that goes beyond a surface understanding?	0 1 2 3 4 5 6
	• Is the content put together in such a way that people understand it?	0 1 2 3 4 5 6
PRESENTATION		
STRUCTURE	• Is there an effective introduction? Are the main ideas clear from the beginning? Is it logical in its organization? Does it naturally flow from one point to another? Does it come to an effective close?	0 1 2 3 4 5 6
ARGUMENT	• Is there enough important detail and evidence to support the claims? Does all information relate to the main idea? Are ideas fully explained and supported with facts, examples, or detail? Is the argument convincing, clear, and logical? Did the speaker understand the topic well enough to transfer that understanding to the audience?	0 1 2 3 4 5 6
REBUTTAL	• Is the rebuttal specific to the opponents' arguments? Are statements clear and concisely worded? Is the rebuttal logical? Does it challenge the opponents' argument?	0 1 2 3 4 5 6
DELIVERY	• Is eye contact made? Are appropriate facial expressions and gestures incorporated? Is the voice clear? Is the speaker poised and excited about the topic? Is the speaker dressed professionally? Are persuasive appeals included? Does the speaker vary pitch and volume? Is the tone clear?	0 1 2 3 4 5 6
CREATIVITY	• Is the content seen in a new way?	0 1 2 3 4 5 6
	• Is the presentation done in a new way?	0 1 2 3 4 5 6
REFLECTION	• What did you learn about the content as you completed this product?	0 1 2 3 4 5 6
	• What did you learn about yourself as a learner by creating this product?	0 1 2 3 4 5 6

Oral Products

Comments

_____

_____

Meaning of Performance Scale:

6—PROFESSIONAL LEVEL: level expected from a professional in the content area

5—ADVANCED LEVEL: level exceeds expectations of the standard

4—PROFICIENT LEVEL: level expected for meeting the standard

3—PROGRESSING LEVEL: level demonstrates movement toward the standard

2—NOVICE LEVEL: level demonstrates initial awareness and knowledge of standard

1—NONPERFORMING LEVEL: level indicates no effort made to meet standard

0—NONPARTICIPATING LEVEL: level indicates nothing turned in

DEBATE Tier 2—DAP TOOL

CONTENT	▪ Content is accurate.	0 1 2 3 4 5 6
	▪ Content has depth and complexity of thought.	0 1 2 3 4 5 6
	▪ Content is organized.	0 1 2 3 4 5 6
PRESENTATION		
STRUCTURE	▪ The opening clearly gains the audience's attention. The main idea is clear and well developed. Strong transitions between main points link to the purpose. It is logical in its organization. The conclusion leaves all questions addressed and impacts the audience.	0 1 2 3 4 5 6
ARGUMENT	▪ Each idea is fully developed and relates strongly to the purpose. A strong balance of general ideas and specific details creates a fluid discussion. All major points are supported by facts, statistics, examples, and logic. Arguments are guided by evidence from credible sources. The speaker understands the essence and nuances of the argument so that it can be fully presented to the audience.	0 1 2 3 4 5 6
REBUTTAL	▪ The rebuttal is clearly directed toward the opponents' arguments. It is logical, concise, and thorough. It challenges opponents' arguments with evidence and facts. It satisfactorily addresses all arguments raised.	0 1 2 3 4 5 6
DELIVERY	▪ Eye contact, facial expressions, and other forms of nonverbal language aid in the audience's understanding and furthers the persuasive purpose. Voice is strong and clear with appropriate intonations. The professionally dressed speaker exhibits enthusiasm and transfers that to the audience. The purposeful use of varied syntax and precise diction appeals to the audience and supports the purpose. Respectful yet persuasive tone is consistent with purpose. Logical, emotional, or ethical persuasive appeals are used.	0 1 2 3 4 5 6
CREATIVITY	▪ Individual insight is expressed in relation to the content.	0 1 2 3 4 5 6
	▪ Individual spark is expressed in relation to the presentation.	0 1 2 3 4 5 6
REFLECTION	▪ Reflection on the learning of the content through product development is apparent.	0 1 2 3 4 5 6
	▪ Reflection on what the student learned about self as a learner is apparent.	0 1 2 3 4 5 6

Comments

_____

_____

Meaning of Performance Scale:

6—PROFESSIONAL LEVEL: level expected from a professional in the content area

5—ADVANCED LEVEL: level exceeds expectations of the standard

4—PROFICIENT LEVEL: level expected for meeting the standard

3—PROGRESSING LEVEL: level demonstrates movement toward the standard

2—NOVICE LEVEL: level demonstrates initial awareness and knowledge of standard

1—NONPERFORMING LEVEL: level indicates no effort made to meet standard

0—NONPARTICIPATING LEVEL: level indicates nothing turned in

DEBATE Tier 3—DAP TOOL

CONTENT		
	▪ Content is accurate and thorough in detail.	0 1 2 3 4 5 6
	▪ Product shows complex understanding and manipulation of content.	0 1 2 3 4 5 6
	▪ Product shows deep probing of content.	0 1 2 3 4 5 6
	▪ Organization is best suited to the product.	0 1 2 3 4 5 6

PRESENTATION

STRUCTURE	▪ The opening cleverly gains the audience's attention. The main idea is original and creative, clearly guiding the entire debate. Sophisticated transitions between main points subtly link all aspects together. Sections fully develop key arguments critical to the purpose. It is ideal in its organization and logic. Closing effectively leaves no question unanswered and ensures the audience understands and agrees.	0 1 2 3 4 5 6
ARGUMENT	▪ Each idea is thoroughly substantiated through pertinent detail, relevant examples, and analyzed support. Strong, elaborate support proves main points. Research shows a deep exploration of relevant literature. The speaker completely understands the main essence and subtle nuances of the argument so that it can be convincingly presented. Audience's possible misunderstandings are clarified. Complex ideas are handled clearly as original interpretations are made.	0 1 2 3 4 5 6
REBUTTAL	▪ The highly logical rebuttal clearly and succinctly addresses all arguments raised. By incorporating specificity and relevance, it effectively challenges opponents' arguments.	0 1 2 3 4 5 6
DELIVERY	▪ Purposeful eye contact, facial expressions, and other forms of nonverbal language enhance the audience's understanding and emphasize the purpose. The strong voice is clear and effective with ideal intonations, volume, and emotion. The professionally dressed speaker exudes enthusiasm for the topic while being totally comfortable in presenting. The purposeful use of varied syntax and powerful diction appeals to the audience and fully supports the purpose. Tone clearly stems from diction, syntax, and figurative language.	0 1 2 3 4 5 6

CREATIVITY		
	▪ Individual insight is originally expressed in relation to the content.	0 1 2 3 4 5 6
	▪ Individual spark is originally expressed in relation to the presentation.	0 1 2 3 4 5 6

REFLECTION		
	▪ Insightful reflection on the learning of the content through product development is expressed.	0 1 2 3 4 5 6
	▪ Insightful reflection on what the student learned about self as a learner is expressed.	0 1 2 3 4 5 6

Oral Products

Comments

Meaning of Performance Scale:

6—PROFESSIONAL LEVEL: level expected from a professional in the content area

5—ADVANCED LEVEL: level exceeds expectations of the standard

4—PROFICIENT LEVEL: level expected for meeting the standard

3—PROGRESSING LEVEL: level demonstrates movement toward the standard

2—NOVICE LEVEL: level demonstrates initial awareness and knowledge of standard

1—NONPERFORMING LEVEL: level indicates no effort made to meet standard

0—NONPARTICIPATING LEVEL: level indicates nothing turned in

INTERVIEW (LIVE)—INTERVIEWER Tier 1—DAP TOOL

CONTENT		• Is the content correct and complete?	0 1 2 3 4 5 6
		• Has the content been thought about in a way that goes beyond a surface understanding?	0 1 2 3 4 5 6
		• Is the content put together in such a way that people understand it?	0 1 2 3 4 5 6
PRESENTATION			
	PURPOSE/ AUDIENCE/SETTING	• Is the purpose clear? Is the person to be interviewed a good choice for the topic? Have you made the interviewee comfortable? Is the setting ready for the interview: Is it quiet? Do you have your materials and equipment ready? Have you practiced with the equipment?	0 1 2 3 4 5 6
	QUESTIONS	• Original: Have you prepared questions that are open ended with no right or wrong answers? Are they important questions that draw out information? Are they worded correctly? Are they limited in number?	0 1 2 3 4 5 6
		• Follow-up: Do you ask the interviewee to expand on or reword an answer if it is unclear? If there is a new idea, do you follow up? Are these questions clear, important to the topic, and worded correctly?	
	FORMAT	• Are you a patient listener? Do you help keep the person on topic? Do you reword your questions if the interviewee is confused or hesitant to answer? Are you clear, concise, and focused? Do you give plenty of time for the interviewee to answer?	0 1 2 3 4 5 6
	WRITTEN COMPONENT (OPTIONAL)	• Have you taken detailed notes in order to write down answers to each question? After the interview, have you rewritten the questions and answers into a dialogue or other appropriate format? If you left out parts of the interview, are you explaining why you have done this? Are the introduction and conclusion strong?	0 1 2 3 4 5 6
CREATIVITY		• Is the content seen in a new way?	0 1 2 3 4 5 6
		• Is the presentation done in a new way?	0 1 2 3 4 5 6
REFLECTION		• What did you learn about the content as you completed this product?	0 1 2 3 4 5 6
		• What did you learn about yourself as a learner by creating this product?	0 1 2 3 4 5 6

Comments

Meaning of Performance Scale:

6—PROFESSIONAL LEVEL: level expected from a professional in the content area

5—ADVANCED LEVEL: level exceeds expectations of the standard

4—PROFICIENT LEVEL: level expected for meeting the standard

3—PROGRESSING LEVEL: level demonstrates movement toward the standard

2—NOVICE LEVEL: level demonstrates initial awareness and knowledge of standard

1—NONPERFORMING LEVEL: level indicates no effort made to meet standard

0—NONPARTICIPATING LEVEL: level indicates nothing turned in

INTERVIEW (LIVE)—INTERVIEWER Tier 2—DAP TOOL

CONTENT	• Content is accurate.	0 1 2 3 4 5 6
	• Content has depth and complexity of thought.	0 1 2 3 4 5 6
	• Content is organized.	0 1 2 3 4 5 6
PRESENTATION		
PURPOSE/ AUDIENCE/SETTING	• The purpose of the interview is clear. The interviewee is highly knowledgeable about the subject. The setting establishes a comfortable environment.	0 1 2 3 4 5 6
QUESTIONS	• Original: Questions are pointed, open ended, and grammatically correct. They cover all main aspects of the topic. • Follow-up: Follow-up questions are appropriate, pointed, and grammatically correct.	0 1 2 3 4 5 6
FORMAT	• The interviewer puts the interviewee at ease through his demeanor, active listening, and clarifying questions.	0 1 2 3 4 5 6
WRITTEN COMPONENT (OPTIONAL)	• The interview, in accurate dialogue form, is thorough and an exact rendering. Any deviations are explained. A strong introduction and conclusion emphasize the purpose.	0 1 2 3 4 5 6
CREATIVITY	• Individual insight is expressed in relation to the content.	0 1 2 3 4 5 6
	• Individual spark is expressed in relation to the presentation.	0 1 2 3 4 5 6
REFLECTION	• Reflection on the learning of the content through product development is apparent.	0 1 2 3 4 5 6
	• Reflection on what the student learned about self as a learner is apparent.	0 1 2 3 4 5 6

Comments

_____

_____

Meaning of Performance Scale:

6—PROFESSIONAL LEVEL: level expected from a professional in the content area

5—ADVANCED LEVEL: level exceeds expectations of the standard

4—PROFICIENT LEVEL: level expected for meeting the standard

3—PROGRESSING LEVEL: level demonstrates movement toward the standard

2—NOVICE LEVEL: level demonstrates initial awareness and knowledge of standard

1—NONPERFORMING LEVEL: level indicates no effort made to meet standard

0—NONPARTICIPATING LEVEL: level indicates nothing turned in

INTERVIEW (LIVE)—INTERVIEWER Tier 3—DAP TOOL

CONTENT	▪ Content is accurate and thorough in detail.	0 1 2 3 4 5 6
	▪ Product shows complex understanding and manipulation of content.	0 1 2 3 4 5 6
	▪ Product shows deep probing of content.	0 1 2 3 4 5 6
	▪ Organization is best suited to the product.	0 1 2 3 4 5 6
PRESENTATION		
PURPOSE/ AUDIENCE/SETTING	▪ The purpose of the interview is woven throughout each exchange. The interviewee is an expert on the topic. The setting purposefully exudes comfort and establishes rapport.	0 1 2 3 4 5 6
QUESTIONS	▪ Original: Questions are exact, probing, open ended, and grammatically correct. They skillfully cover all main aspects of the topic. ▪ Follow-up: Follow-up questions are insightful, probing, pointed, and grammatically correct.	0 1 2 3 4 5 6
FORMAT	▪ The interviewer naturally puts the interviewee at ease through demeanor, active listening, and clarifying questions.	0 1 2 3 4 5 6
WRITTEN COMPONENT (OPTIONAL)	▪ The piece perfectly mirrors the interview in dialogue form. Any deviations are purposeful and fully explained. The introduction and conclusion expertly enhance the purpose.	0 1 2 3 4 5 6
CREATIVITY	▪ Individual insight is originally expressed in relation to the content.	0 1 2 3 4 5 6
	▪ Individual spark is originally expressed in relation to the presentation.	0 1 2 3 4 5 6
REFLECTION	▪ Insightful reflection on the learning of the content through product development is expressed.	0 1 2 3 4 5 6
	▪ Insightful reflection on what the student learned about self as a learner is expressed.	0 1 2 3 4 5 6

Comments

_____

_____

Meaning of Performance Scale:

6—PROFESSIONAL LEVEL: level expected from a professional in the content area

5—ADVANCED LEVEL: level exceeds expectations of the standard

4—PROFICIENT LEVEL: level expected for meeting the standard

3—PROGRESSING LEVEL: level demonstrates movement toward the standard

2—NOVICE LEVEL: level demonstrates initial awareness and knowledge of standard

1—NONPERFORMING LEVEL: level indicates no effort made to meet standard

0—NONPARTICIPATING LEVEL: level indicates nothing turned in

INTERVIEW (LIVE)—INTERVIEWEE Tier 1—DAP TOOL

CONTENT	▪ Is the content correct and complete?	0 1 2 3 4 5 6
	▪ Has the content been thought about in a way that goes beyond a surface understanding?	0 1 2 3 4 5 6
	▪ Is the content put together in such a way that people understand it?	0 1 2 3 4 5 6
PRESENTATION		
PREPARATION	▪ Have you researched the topic well so that you can answer questions?	0 1 2 3 4 5 6
ANSWERS	▪ Do you answer the questions asked? Are you correct? Do you give detail? Do you question the interviewer if you don't understand a question?	0 1 2 3 4 5 6
TECHNIQUE	▪ Are you making eye contact and really listening to the questions? Does your body language send the message that you are interested? Is your voice easy to hear?	0 1 2 3 4 5 6
CREATIVITY	▪ Is the content seen in a new way?	0 1 2 3 4 5 6
	▪ Is the presentation done in a new way?	0 1 2 3 4 5 6
REFLECTION	▪ What did you learn about the content as you completed this product?	0 1 2 3 4 5 6
	▪ What did you learn about yourself as a learner by creating this product?	0 1 2 3 4 5 6

Comments

Meaning of Performance Scale:

6—PROFESSIONAL LEVEL: level expected from a professional in the content area

5—ADVANCED LEVEL: level exceeds expectations of the standard

4—PROFICIENT LEVEL: level expected for meeting the standard

3—PROGRESSING LEVEL: level demonstrates movement toward the standard

2—NOVICE LEVEL: level demonstrates initial awareness and knowledge of standard

1—NONPERFORMING LEVEL: level indicates no effort made to meet standard

0—NONPARTICIPATING LEVEL: level indicates nothing turned in

INTERVIEW (LIVE)—INTERVIEWEE Tier 2—DAP TOOL

CONTENT	▪ Content is accurate.	0 1 2 3 4 5 6
	▪ Content has depth and complexity of thought.	0 1 2 3 4 5 6
	▪ Content is organized.	0 1 2 3 4 5 6
PRESENTATION		
PREPARATION	▪ Topic has been well researched.	0 1 2 3 4 5 6
ANSWERS	▪ Strong, complete, and accurate answers are given to each question. The interviewee asked for clarification when needed.	0 1 2 3 4 5 6
TECHNIQUE	▪ Active listening skills are used. Gestures and facial expressions indicate deep interest and enthusiasm. The voice is strong and confident, the tone positive.	0 1 2 3 4 5 6
CREATIVITY	▪ Individual insight is expressed in relation to the content.	0 1 2 3 4 5 6
	▪ Individual spark is expressed in relation to the presentation.	0 1 2 3 4 5 6
REFLECTION	▪ Reflection on the learning of the content through product development is apparent.	0 1 2 3 4 5 6
	▪ Reflection on what the student learned about self as a learner is apparent.	0 1 2 3 4 5 6

Comments

_____

_____

Meaning of Performance Scale:

6—PROFESSIONAL LEVEL: level expected from a professional in the content area

5—ADVANCED LEVEL: level exceeds expectations of the standard

4—PROFICIENT LEVEL: level expected for meeting the standard

3—PROGRESSING LEVEL: level demonstrates movement toward the standard

2—NOVICE LEVEL: level demonstrates initial awareness and knowledge of standard

1—NONPERFORMING LEVEL: level indicates no effort made to meet standard

0—NONPARTICIPATING LEVEL: level indicates nothing turned in

INTERVIEW (LIVE)—INTERVIEWEE Tier 3—DAP TOOL

CONTENT	▪ Content is accurate and thorough in detail.	0 1 2 3 4 5 6
	▪ Product shows complex understanding and manipulation of content.	0 1 2 3 4 5 6
	▪ Product shows deep probing of content.	0 1 2 3 4 5 6
	▪ Organization is best suited to the product.	0 1 2 3 4 5 6
PRESENTATION		
PREPARATION	▪ Topic has been thoroughly researched and analyzed.	0 1 2 3 4 5 6
ANSWERS	▪ Detailed, comprehensive answers are given. The interviewee feels free to ask purposeful questions for clarification and understanding.	0 1 2 3 4 5 6
TECHNIQUE	▪ A strong rapport is established between interviewer and interviewee. Intent, active listening coupled with positive nonverbals help support the exchange of ideas.	0 1 2 3 4 5 6
CREATIVITY	▪ Individual insight is originally expressed in relation to the content.	0 1 2 3 4 5 6
	▪ Individual spark is originally expressed in relation to the presentation.	0 1 2 3 4 5 6
REFLECTION	▪ Insightful reflection on the learning of the content through product development is expressed.	0 1 2 3 4 5 6
	▪ Insightful reflection on what the student learned about self as a learner is expressed.	0 1 2 3 4 5 6

Comments

_____

_____

Meaning of Performance Scale:

6—PROFESSIONAL LEVEL: level expected from a professional in the content area

5—ADVANCED LEVEL: level exceeds expectations of the standard

4—PROFICIENT LEVEL: level expected for meeting the standard

3—PROGRESSING LEVEL: level demonstrates movement toward the standard

2—NOVICE LEVEL: level demonstrates initial awareness and knowledge of standard

1—NONPERFORMING LEVEL: level indicates no effort made to meet standard

0—NONPARTICIPATING LEVEL: level indicates nothing turned in

INTERVIEW (RECORDED) Tier 1—DAP TOOL

CONTENT	• Is the content correct and complete?	0 1 2 3 4 5 6
	• Has the content been thought about in a way that goes beyond a surface understanding?	0 1 2 3 4 5 6
	• Is the content put together in such a way that people understand it?	0 1 2 3 4 5 6
PRESENTATION		
PURPOSE/ AUDIENCE/SETTING	• Is the purpose clear? Is the person to be interviewed a good choice for the topic? Have you made the interviewee comfortable? Is the setting quiet and ready for the interview? Do you have your materials and equipment ready? Have you practiced with the equipment?	0 1 2 3 4 5 6
QUESTIONS	• Original: Have you prepared questions that are open ended with no right or wrong answers? Are they important questions that draw out information? Are they worded correctly? Are they limited in number?	0 1 2 3 4 5 6
	• Follow-up: Do you ask the interviewee to expand on or reword an answer if it is unclear? If there is a new idea, do you follow up? Are these questions clear, important to the topic, and worded correctly?	
	• Technique: Are you a patient listener? Do you keep the person on topic? Do you reword your questions if the interviewee is confused or hesitant to answer? Are you clear, concise, and focused on your main topic? Do you give plenty of time for the interviewee to answer?	
FORMAT	• Is the audio or video recording clear and easy to hear? Do you use a voice that encourages answers? Does your body language show that you are interested? Do you summarize what you discovered about your topic?	0 1 2 3 4 5 6
CREATIVITY	• Is the content seen in a new way?	0 1 2 3 4 5 6
	• Is the presentation done in a new way?	0 1 2 3 4 5 6
REFLECTION	• What did you learn about the content as you completed this product?	0 1 2 3 4 5 6
	• What did you learn about yourself as a learner by creating this product?	0 1 2 3 4 5 6

Comments

_____

_____

Meaning of Performance Scale:

6—PROFESSIONAL LEVEL: level expected from a professional in the content area

5—ADVANCED LEVEL: level exceeds expectations of the standard

4—PROFICIENT LEVEL: level expected for meeting the standard

3—PROGRESSING LEVEL: level demonstrates movement toward the standard

2—NOVICE LEVEL: level demonstrates initial awareness and knowledge of standard

1—NONPERFORMING LEVEL: level indicates no effort made to meet standard

0—NONPARTICIPATING LEVEL: level indicates nothing turned in

INTERVIEW (RECORDED) Tier 2—DAP TOOL

CONTENT	▪ Content is accurate.	0 1 2 3 4 5 6
	▪ Content has depth and complexity of thought.	0 1 2 3 4 5 6
	▪ Content is organized.	0 1 2 3 4 5 6
PRESENTATION		
PURPOSE/ AUDIENCE/SETTING	▪ The purpose of the interview is clear. The interviewee is highly knowledgeable about the subject. The setting establishes a comfortable environment.	0 1 2 3 4 5 6
QUESTIONS	▪ Original: Questions are pointed, open ended, and grammatically correct. They cover all main aspects of the topic. ▪ Follow-up: Follow-up questions are appropriate, pointed, and grammatically correct. ▪ Technique: The interviewer puts the interviewee at ease through demeanor, active listening, and clarifying questions.	0 1 2 3 4 5 6
FORMAT	▪ The audio or video recording does not detract from the interview. The interviewer's tone and nonverbal language demonstrate interest and encouragement.	0 1 2 3 4 5 6
CREATIVITY	▪ Individual insight is expressed in relation to the content.	0 1 2 3 4 5
	▪ Individual spark is expressed in relation to the presentation.	0 1 2 3 4 5 6
REFLECTION	▪ Reflection on the learning of the content through product development is apparent.	0 1 2 3 4 5 6
	▪ Reflection on what the student learned about self as a learner is apparent.	0 1 2 3 4 5 6

Comments

_____

_____

Meaning of Performance Scale:

6—PROFESSIONAL LEVEL: level expected from a professional in the content area

5—ADVANCED LEVEL: level exceeds expectations of the standard

4—PROFICIENT LEVEL: level expected for meeting the standard

3—PROGRESSING LEVEL: level demonstrates movement toward the standard

2—NOVICE LEVEL: level demonstrates initial awareness and knowledge of standard

1—NONPERFORMING LEVEL: level indicates no effort made to meet standard

0—NONPARTICIPATING LEVEL: level indicates nothing turned in

INTERVIEW (RECORDED) Tier 3—DAP TOOL

CONTENT	• Content is accurate and thorough in detail.	0 1 2 3 4 5 6
	• Product shows complex understanding and manipulation of content.	0 1 2 3 4 5 6
	• Product shows deep probing of content.	0 1 2 3 4 5 6
	• Organization is best suited to the product.	0 1 2 3 4 5 6
PRESENTATION		
PURPOSE/ AUDIENCE/SETTING	• The purpose of the interview is woven throughout each exchange. The interviewee is an expert on the topic. The setting purposefully exudes comfort and establishes rapport.	0 1 2 3 4 5 6
QUESTIONS	• Original: Questions are exact, probing, open ended, and grammatically correct. They skillfully cover all main aspects of the topic. • Follow-up: Follow-up questions are insightful, probing, pointed, and grammatically correct. • Technique: The interviewer naturally puts the interviewee at ease through demeanor, active listening, and clarifying questions.	0 1 2 3 4 5 6
FORMAT	• The audio or video recording is clear and well recorded. The interviewer's tone purposefully builds a comfortable rapport. Nonverbal language is deliberate and encouraging.	0 1 2 3 4 5 6
CREATIVITY	• Individual insight is originally expressed in relation to the content.	0 1 2 3 4 5 6
	• Individual spark is originally expressed in relation to the presentation.	0 1 2 3 4 5 6
REFLECTION	• Insightful reflection on the learning of the content through product development is expressed.	0 1 2 3 4 5 6
	• Insightful reflection on what the student learned about self as a learner is expressed.	0 1 2 3 4 5 6

Comments

Meaning of Performance Scale:

6—PROFESSIONAL LEVEL: level expected from a professional in the content area

5—ADVANCED LEVEL: level exceeds expectations of the standard

4—PROFICIENT LEVEL: level expected for meeting the standard

3—PROGRESSING LEVEL: level demonstrates movement toward the standard

2—NOVICE LEVEL: level demonstrates initial awareness and knowledge of standard

1—NONPERFORMING LEVEL: level indicates no effort made to meet standard

0—NONPARTICIPATING LEVEL: level indicates nothing turned in

MONOLOGUE Tier 1—DAP TOOL

CONTENT	▪ Is the content correct and complete?	0 1 2 3 4 5 6
	▪ Has the content been thought about in a way that goes beyond a surface understanding?	0 1 2 3 4 5 6
	▪ Is the content put together in such a way that people understand it?	0 1 2 3 4 5 6
PRESENTATION		
SCRIPT	▪ Is the script clear and written for a specific audience? Is the purpose clear?	0 1 2 3 4 5 6
CHARACTERIZATION	▪ Does the speaker create a clear character?	0 1 2 3 4 5 6
VOICE	▪ Is the voice easily heard? Is the tone appropriate?	0 1 2 3 4 5 6
GESTURES	▪ Are gestures appropriate to the character?	0 1 2 3 4 5 6
CREATIVITY	▪ Is the content seen in a new way?	0 1 2 3 4 5 6
	▪ Is the presentation done in a new way?	0 1 2 3 4 5 6
REFLECTION	▪ What did you learn about the content as you completed this product?	0 1 2 3 4 5 6
	▪ What did you learn about yourself as a learner by creating this product?	0 1 2 3 4 5 6

Comments

_____

_____

Meaning of Performance Scale:

6—PROFESSIONAL LEVEL: level expected from a professional in the content area

5—ADVANCED LEVEL: level exceeds expectations of the standard

4—PROFICIENT LEVEL: level expected for meeting the standard

3—PROGRESSING LEVEL: level demonstrates movement toward the standard

2—NOVICE LEVEL: level demonstrates initial awareness and knowledge of standard

1—NONPERFORMING LEVEL: level indicates no effort made to meet standard

0—NONPARTICIPATING LEVEL: level indicates nothing turned in

Note. Adapted from *Strategies for Differentiating Instruction: Best Practices for the Classroom* (p. 205), by J. L. Roberts and T. F. Inman, 2007, Waco, TX: Prufrock Press. Copyright © 2007 by Prufrock Press. Adapted with permission.

MONOLOGUE Tier 2—DAP TOOL

CONTENT		
	▪ Content is accurate.	0 1 2 3 4 5 6
	▪ Content has depth and complexity of thought.	0 1 2 3 4 5 6
	▪ Content is organized.	0 1 2 3 4 5 6
PRESENTATION		
SCRIPT	▪ Script is clear, interesting, and designed for the audience as to word choice and purpose.	0 1 2 3 4 5 6
CHARACTERIZATION	▪ The speaker creates a believable character.	0 1 2 3 4 5 6
VOICE	▪ Voice enhances characterization through quality, tone, and emphasis.	0 1 2 3 4 5 6
GESTURES	▪ Gestures, including body language, are consistent with the character.	0 1 2 3 4 5 6
CREATIVITY	▪ Individual insight is expressed in relation to the content.	0 1 2 3 4 5 6
	▪ Individual spark is expressed in relation to the presentation.	0 1 2 3 4 5 6
REFLECTION	▪ Reflection on the learning of the content through product development is apparent.	0 1 2 3 4 5 6
	▪ Reflection on what the student learned about self as a learner is apparent.	0 1 2 3 4 5 6

Comments

Meaning of Performance Scale:

6—PROFESSIONAL LEVEL: level expected from a professional in the content area

5—ADVANCED LEVEL: level exceeds expectations of the standard

4—PROFICIENT LEVEL: level expected for meeting the standard

3—PROGRESSING LEVEL: level demonstrates movement toward the standard

2—NOVICE LEVEL: level demonstrates initial awareness and knowledge of standard

1—NONPERFORMING LEVEL: level indicates no effort made to meet standard

0—NONPARTICIPATING LEVEL: level indicates nothing turned in

Note. Adapted from *Strategies for Differentiating Instruction: Best Practices for the Classroom* (p. 206), by J. L. Roberts and T. F. Inman, 2007, Waco, TX: Prufrock Press. Copyright © 2007 by Prufrock Press. Adapted with permission.

MONOLOGUE Tier 3—DAP TOOL

CONTENT	▪ Content is accurate and thorough in detail.	0 1 2 3 4 5 6
	▪ Product shows complex understanding and manipulation of content.	0 1 2 3 4 5 6
	▪ Product shows deep probing of content.	0 1 2 3 4 5 6
	▪ Organization is best suited to the product.	0 1 2 3 4 5 6
PRESENTATION		
SCRIPT	▪ Script flows, moving easily from beginning to the body to the ending, plus the diction and syntax enhance the audience's understanding.	0 1 2 3 4 5 6
CHARACTERIZATION	▪ The speaker maintains persona throughout performance.	0 1 2 3 4 5 6
VOICE	▪ Voice effectively uses inflection, varies pace, and employs pauses to enhance performance and improve meaning.	0 1 2 3 4 5 6
GESTURES	▪ Gestures, including body language, enhance the performance and improve meaning.	0 1 2 3 4 5 6
CREATIVITY	▪ Individual insight is originally expressed in relation to the content.	0 1 2 3 4 5 6
	▪ Individual spark is originally expressed in relation to the presentation.	0 1 2 3 4 5 6
REFLECTION	▪ Insightful reflection on the learning of the content through product development is expressed.	0 1 2 3 4 5 6
	▪ Insightful reflection on what the student learned about self as a learner is expressed.	0 1 2 3 4 5 6

Comments

_____

_____

Meaning of Performance Scale:

6—PROFESSIONAL LEVEL: level expected from a professional in the content area

5—ADVANCED LEVEL: level exceeds expectations of the standard

4—PROFICIENT LEVEL: level expected for meeting the standard

3—PROGRESSING LEVEL: level demonstrates movement toward the standard

2—NOVICE LEVEL: level demonstrates initial awareness and knowledge of standard

1—NONPERFORMING LEVEL: level indicates no effort made to meet standard

0—NONPARTICIPATING LEVEL: level indicates nothing turned in

Note. Adapted from *Strategies for Differentiating Instruction: Best Practices for the Classroom* (p. 207), by J. L. Roberts and T. F. Inman, 2007, Waco, TX: Prufrock Press. Copyright © 2007 by Prufrock Press. Adapted with permission.

ORAL REPORT/PRESENTATION Tier 1—DAP TOOL

CONTENT	▪ Is the content correct and complete?	0 1 2 3 4 5 6
	▪ Has the content been thought about in a way that goes beyond a surface understanding?	0 1 2 3 4 5 6
	▪ Is the content put together in such a way that people understand it?	0 1 2 3 4 5 6
PRESENTATION		
STRUCTURE	▪ Is an effective attention-getting device used? Is the topic clear from the beginning? Is the presentation logical in its organization? Does one major idea naturally flow to another? Does it come to an effective close?	0 1 2 3 4 5 6
ELABORATION AND SUPPORT	▪ Does all information relate to the main idea? Are ideas fully explained and supported with evidence? If outside sources are used, have they been used carefully and appropriately? Does the audience leave with new insight?	0 1 2 3 4 5 6
DELIVERY	▪ Is the presentation developed for the expected audience and purpose through its word choice, sentence structure, and tone? Is eye contact maintained? Are appropriate expressions and gestures incorporated? Is the voice clear? Is the speaker poised and comfortable? If notes are used, are they only briefly referred to if at all? Has the material been prepared for an oral, not a written, presentation?	0 1 2 3 4 5 6
PROFESSIONALISM	▪ Has the presentation been well prepared? Is the speaker appropriately dressed? Has time been utilized efficiently? Does the speaker modify or clarify the material based on the audience's needs? Does he answer all questions effectively?	0 1 2 3 4 5 6
COMMUNICATION DEVICES (OPTIONAL)	▪ Do communication devices (e.g., graphics, visual aids, handouts, etc.) enhance the presentation? Are they of high quality and easy for the audience to see and understand? Is there an appropriate use of media?	0 1 2 3 4 5 6
CREATIVITY	▪ Is the content seen in a new way?	0 1 2 3 4 5 6
	▪ Is the presentation done in a new way?	0 1 2 3 4 5 6
REFLECTION	▪ What did you learn about the content as you completed this product?	0 1 2 3 4 5 6
	▪ What did you learn about yourself as a learner by creating this product?	0 1 2 3 4 5 6

Comments

Meaning of Performance Scale:

6—PROFESSIONAL LEVEL: level expected from a professional in the content area

5—ADVANCED LEVEL: level exceeds expectations of the standard

4—PROFICIENT LEVEL: level expected for meeting the standard

3—PROGRESSING LEVEL: level demonstrates movement toward the standard

2—NOVICE LEVEL: level demonstrates initial awareness and knowledge of standard

1—NONPERFORMING LEVEL: level indicates no effort made to meet standard

0—NONPARTICIPATING LEVEL: level indicates nothing turned in

ORAL REPORT/PRESENTATION Tier 2—DAP TOOL

CONTENT	▪ Content is accurate.	0 1 2 3 4 5 6
	▪ Content has depth and complexity of thought.	0 1 2 3 4 5 6
	▪ Content is organized.	0 1 2 3 4 5 6
PRESENTATION		
STRUCTURE	▪ The attention-getting device clearly gains the audience's attention. The main idea is clear and well developed. Strong transitions between main points link to the purpose. The presentation is logical in its organization. The conclusion pulls all aspects together and comes to a strong closure.	0 1 2 3 4 5 6
ELABORATION AND SUPPORT	▪ Each idea is fully developed and relates to the purpose. A strong balance of general ideas and specific details creates a fluid discussion. Quotations or other references, if used, fully elaborate on or support the main points and are smoothly incorporated. The audience leaves with new insight and perspective on the topic.	0 1 2 3 4 5 6
DELIVERY	▪ The purposeful use of varied syntax and precise diction aids in the audience's understanding. Tone is consistent with purpose. Eye contact, facial expressions, and other forms of nonverbal communication aid in the audience's understanding, gain their trust, and further the purpose. Speaker's voice is strong and clear with appropriate intonations and pronunciations. Speaker exhibits confidence yet stirs interest in the audience. Notes are used minimally. Material has purposefully been prepared for an oral, not a written, presentation.	0 1 2 3 4 5 6
PROFESSIONALISM	▪ Presentation is well prepared. The speaker dresses professionally and uses time effectively. The speaker, paying close attention to his audience, modifies, clarifies, or adds to the information as needed. He addresses all questions and concerns effectively and respectfully.	0 1 2 3 4 5 6
COMMUNICATION DEVICES (OPTIONAL)	▪ Communication devices (e.g., graphics, visual aids, handouts) enhance the presentation and increase understanding. They are high quality, visible, and readily understandable. Varied use of media enhances the devices.	0 1 2 3 4 5 6
CREATIVITY	▪ Individual insight is expressed in relation to the content.	0 1 2 3 4 5 6
	▪ Individual spark is expressed in relation to the presentation.	0 1 2 3 4 5 6
REFLECTION	▪ Reflection on the learning of the content through product development is apparent.	0 1 2 3 4 5 6
	▪ Reflection on what the student learned about self as a learner is apparent.	0 1 2 3 4 5 6

Comments

Meaning of Performance Scale:

6—PROFESSIONAL LEVEL: level expected from a professional in the content area

5—ADVANCED LEVEL: level exceeds expectations of the standard

4—PROFICIENT LEVEL: level expected for meeting the standard

3—PROGRESSING LEVEL: level demonstrates movement toward the standard

2—NOVICE LEVEL: level demonstrates initial awareness and knowledge of standard

1—NONPERFORMING LEVEL: level indicates no effort made to meet standard

0—NONPARTICIPATING LEVEL: level indicates nothing turned in

ORAL REPORT/PRESENTATION Tier 3—DAP TOOL

CONTENT	▪ Content is accurate and thorough in detail.	0 1 2 3 4 5 6
	▪ Product shows complex understanding and manipulation of content.	0 1 2 3 4 5 6
	▪ Product shows deep probing of content.	0 1 2 3 4 5 6
	▪ Organization is best suited to the product.	0 1 2 3 4 5 6

PRESENTATION		
STRUCTURE	▪ The attention-getting device cleverly gains the audience's attention. The main idea is original and creative, clearly guiding the entire presentation. Sophisticated transitions between main points subtly link all aspects together. Sections fully develop key concepts or ideas critical to the purpose. It is ideal in its organization. Conclusion emphasizes main ideas and is significant.	0 1 2 3 4 5 6
ELABORATION AND SUPPORT	▪ Each idea is thoroughly substantiated through pertinent detail or analyzed support from a variety of sources. Quotations or other references fully elaborate on or support the idea; their inclusion is seamless. The presentation anticipates the audience's possible misunderstandings and handles complex ideas clearly. The audience leaves enlightened.	0 1 2 3 4 5 6
DELIVERY	▪ The intentional use of varied syntax and powerful diction enhances audience's understanding. Effective rhetorical devices emphasize main ideas. Purposeful eye contact, facial expressions, and other forms of nonverbal communication enhance the audience's understanding and emphasize the purpose. Speaker's voice is strong, clear, and effective. Speaker exudes passion for the topic while being in total control of the presentation and audience. No notes are used. Material is best suited for an oral, not a written, presentation.	0 1 2 3 4 5 6
PROFESSIONALISM	▪ Time and effort in preparation are evident. Meticulous attention has been paid to dressing professionally and using allotted time wisely. The speaker intuitively meets his audience's needs by modifying the material as needed. In a nonpatronizing manner, he answers and even anticipates questions from the audience.	0 1 2 3 4 5 6
COMMUNICATION DEVICES (OPTIONAL)	▪ Communication devices (e.g., graphics, visual aids, handouts) optimize the presentation, increasing understanding and emphasizing main points. Looking professional, they are visible and engaging to all. The media of the device best matches its purpose.	0 1 2 3 4 5 6

CREATIVITY	▪ Individual insight is originally expressed in relation to the content.	0 1 2 3 4 5 6
	▪ Individual spark is originally expressed in relation to the presentation.	0 1 2 3 4 5 6

REFLECTION	▪ Insightful reflection on the learning of the content through product development is expressed.	0 1 2 3 4 5 6
	▪ Insightful reflection on what the student learned about self as a learner is expressed.	0 1 2 3 4 5 6

Comments

_____

_____

Meaning of Performance Scale:

6—PROFESSIONAL LEVEL: level expected from a professional in the content area

5—ADVANCED LEVEL: level exceeds expectations of the standard

4—PROFICIENT LEVEL: level expected for meeting the standard

3—PROGRESSING LEVEL: level demonstrates movement toward the standard

2—NOVICE LEVEL: level demonstrates initial awareness and knowledge of standard

1—NONPERFORMING LEVEL: level indicates no effort made to meet standard

0—NONPARTICIPATING LEVEL: level indicates nothing turned in

SPEECH (ORAL) Tier 1—DAP TOOL

CONTENT	▪ Is the content correct and complete?	0 1 2 3 4 5 6
	▪ Has the content been thought about in a way that goes beyond a surface understanding?	0 1 2 3 4 5 6
	▪ Is the content put together in such a way that people understand it?	0 1 2 3 4 5 6
PRESENTATION		
STRUCTURE	▪ Is an effective attention-getting device used? Is the main idea clear from the beginning? Is the speech logical in its organization, naturally flowing from one major idea to another? Does it come to an effective close?	0 1 2 3 4 5 6
ELABORATION AND SUPPORT	▪ Does all information relate to the main idea? Are ideas fully explained and supported? Is there a balance of general ideas with specific details? If quotations or other references are used, have they been used carefully and appropriately?	0 1 2 3 4 5 6
DELIVERY	▪ Is eye contact made? Are appropriate facial expressions and gestures incorporated? Is the speaker's voice clear? Is the speaker poised and comfortable? If notes are used, are they only briefly referred to if at all?	0 1 2 3 4 5 6
STYLE	▪ Is the speech developed for the expected audience and purpose? Are appropriate words used? Are the sentences varied in structure? Is a suitable tone used? Is figurative language used in an effective way?	0 1 2 3 4 5 6
CREATIVITY	▪ Is the content seen in a new way?	0 1 2 3 4 5 6
	▪ Is the presentation done in a new way?	0 1 2 3 4 5 6
REFLECTION	▪ What did you learn about the content as you completed this product?	0 1 2 3 4 5 6
	▪ What did you learn about yourself as a learner by creating this product?	0 1 2 3 4 5 6

Comments

_____

_____

Meaning of Performance Scale:

6—PROFESSIONAL LEVEL: level expected from a professional in the content area

5—ADVANCED LEVEL: level exceeds expectations of the standard

4—PROFICIENT LEVEL: level expected for meeting the standard

3—PROGRESSING LEVEL: level demonstrates movement toward the standard

2—NOVICE LEVEL: level demonstrates initial awareness and knowledge of standard

1—NONPERFORMING LEVEL: level indicates no effort made to meet standard

0—NONPARTICIPATING LEVEL: level indicates nothing turned in

SPEECH (ORAL) Tier 2—DAP TOOL

CONTENT	▪ Content is accurate.	0 1 2 3 4 5 6
	▪ Content has depth and complexity of thought.	0 1 2 3 4 5 6
	▪ Content is organized.	0 1 2 3 4 5 6
PRESENTATION		
STRUCTURE	▪ The attention-getting device clearly gains the audience's attention. The main idea is clear and well developed. Strong transitions between main points link to the purpose and any narrative threads. The speech is logical in its organization. The conclusion, pulling together all aspects, comes to a strong closure.	0 1 2 3 4 5 6
ELABORATION AND SUPPORT	▪ Each idea is fully developed and relates to the purpose. A strong balance of general ideas and specific details creates a fluid discussion. Quotations or other references, if used, fully elaborate on or support the main points and are smoothly incorporated.	0 1 2 3 4 5 6
DELIVERY	▪ Eye contact, facial expressions, and other forms of nonverbal communication aid in the audience's understanding and further the purpose. Speaker's voice is strong and clear with appropriate intonations. Speaker exhibits calm yet stirs interest in the audience. Notes are used minimally if at all.	0 1 2 3 4 5 6
STYLE	▪ The purposeful use of varied syntax and precise diction aids in the audience's understanding. Tone is consistent with purpose. Voice clearly stems from diction, syntax, and figurative language. Ethos is strongly realized in the audience.	0 1 2 3 4 5 6
CREATIVITY	▪ Individual insight is expressed in relation to the content.	0 1 2 3 4 5 6
	▪ Individual spark is expressed in relation to the presentation.	0 1 2 3 4 5 6
REFLECTION	▪ Reflection on the learning of the content through product development is apparent.	0 1 2 3 4 5 6
	▪ Reflection on what the student learned about self as a learner is apparent.	0 1 2 3 4 5 6

Comments

_____

_____

Meaning of Performance Scale:

6—PROFESSIONAL LEVEL: level expected from a professional in the content area

5—ADVANCED LEVEL: level exceeds expectations of the standard

4—PROFICIENT LEVEL: level expected for meeting the standard

3—PROGRESSING LEVEL: level demonstrates movement toward the standard

2—NOVICE LEVEL: level demonstrates initial awareness and knowledge of standard

1—NONPERFORMING LEVEL: level indicates no effort made to meet standard

0—NONPARTICIPATING LEVEL: level indicates nothing turned in

SPEECH (ORAL) Tier 3—DAP TOOL

CONTENT	▪ Content is accurate and thorough in detail.	0 1 2 3 4 5 6
	▪ Product shows complex understanding and manipulation of content.	0 1 2 3 4 5 6
	▪ Product shows deep probing of content.	0 1 2 3 4 5 6
	▪ Organization is best suited to the product.	0 1 2 3 4 5 6
PRESENTATION *STRUCTURE*	▪ The attention-getting device cleverly and uniquely gains the audience's interest and provides a thoughtful transition to the thesis. The original and creative thesis guides the entire speech with a coherent narrative thread. Sophisticated transitions subtly link all aspects together. Secondary arguments fully develop key concepts or ideas critical to the purpose. The speech is ideally organized. Conclusion emphasizes pertinent information. The significance of the conclusion is clear.	0 1 2 3 4 5 6
ELABORATION AND SUPPORT	▪ Each idea is thoroughly substantiated through pertinent detail or analyzed support from a variety of sources. Pertinent quotations and other references fully elaborate on or support the idea; their inclusion is seamless. The speech anticipates audience's possible misunderstandings and handles complex ideas clearly.	0 1 2 3 4 5 6
DELIVERY	▪ Purposeful eye contact, facial expressions, and other forms of nonverbal communication enhance the audience's understanding and emphasize the purpose. Speaker's voice is strong, clear, and effective. Speaker exudes passion for the topic while being in total control of the presentation and audience. No notes are used.	0 1 2 3 4 5 6
STYLE	▪ The purposeful use of varied syntax and diction enhances audience's understanding. Tone clearly stems from diction, syntax, and figurative language. Effective rhetorical devices emphasize thesis.	0 1 2 3 4 5 6
CREATIVITY	▪ Individual insight is originally expressed in relation to the content.	0 1 2 3 4 5 6
	▪ Individual spark is originally expressed in relation to the presentation.	0 1 2 3 4 5 6
REFLECTION	▪ Insightful reflection on the learning of the content through product development is expressed.	0 1 2 3 4 5 6
	▪ Insightful reflection on what the student learned about self as a learner is expressed.	0 1 2 3 4 5 6

Oral Products

Comments

_____

_____

Meaning of Performance Scale:
6—PROFESSIONAL LEVEL: level expected from a professional in the content area
5—ADVANCED LEVEL: level exceeds expectations of the standard
4—PROFICIENT LEVEL: level expected for meeting the standard
3—PROGRESSING LEVEL: level demonstrates movement toward the standard
2—NOVICE LEVEL: level demonstrates initial awareness and knowledge of standard
1—NONPERFORMING LEVEL: level indicates no effort made to meet standard
0—NONPARTICIPATING LEVEL: level indicates nothing turned in

COMPUTER GRAPHIC Tier 1—DAP TOOL

CONTENT		• Is the content correct and complete?	0 1 2 3 4 5 6
		• Has the content been thought about in a way that goes beyond a surface understanding?	0 1 2 3 4 5 6
		• Is the content put together in such a way that people understand it?	0 1 2 3 4 5 6
PRESENTATION			
	CONCEPT	• Is the purpose clear? Does the piece appeal to the target audience?	0 1 2 3 4 5 6
	ELEMENTS AND PRINCIPLES OF DESIGN	• Are the elements of design effectively included, especially line, shape, color, and/or value? Are the principles of design effectively included, especially proportion, balance, contrast, rhythm, and/or unity?	0 1 2 3 4 5 6
	TECHNOLOGY	• Has there been a deliberate manipulation of image editing tools? Have professional graphics applications been used in an effective way? Is it multilayered?	0 1 2 3 4 5 6
CREATIVITY		• Is the content seen in a new way?	0 1 2 3 4 5 6
		• Is the presentation done in a new way?	0 1 2 3 4 5 6
REFLECTION		• What did you learn about the content as you completed this product?	0 1 2 3 4 5 6
		• What did you learn about yourself as a learner by creating this product?	0 1 2 3 4 5 6

Comments

_____

_____

Meaning of Performance Scale:

6—PROFESSIONAL LEVEL: level expected from a professional in the content area

5—ADVANCED LEVEL: level exceeds expectations of the standard

4—PROFICIENT LEVEL: level expected for meeting the standard

3—PROGRESSING LEVEL: level demonstrates movement toward the standard

2—NOVICE LEVEL: level demonstrates initial awareness and knowledge of standard

1—NONPERFORMING LEVEL: level indicates no effort made to meet standard

0—NONPARTICIPATING LEVEL: level indicates nothing turned in

COMPUTER GRAPHIC Tier 2—DAP TOOL

CONTENT	• Content is accurate.	0 1 2 3 4 5 6
	• Content has depth and complexity of thought.	0 1 2 3 4 5 6
	• Content is organized.	0 1 2 3 4 5 6
PRESENTATION		
CONCEPT	• The graphic evokes emotions, moods, and/or thoughts in the target audience. The viewers see the purpose clearly.	0 1 2 3 4 5 6
ELEMENTS AND PRINCIPLES OF DESIGN	• Design elements (i.e., line, shape, color, and value) have been carefully considered and integrated. Design principles (especially proportion, balance, contrast, rhythm, and unity) have been successfully integrated.	0 1 2 3 4 5 6
TECHNOLOGY	• A deliberate and successful manipulation of tools has generated a graphic in a nonconventional and interesting way. Professional graphics applications have been used in an innovative way. Skillful multilayering is evident.	0 1 2 3 4 5 6
CREATIVITY	• Individual insight is expressed in relation to the content.	0 1 2 3 4 5 6
	• Individual spark is expressed in relation to the presentation.	0 1 2 3 4 5 6
REFLECTION	• Reflection on the learning of the content through product development is apparent.	0 1 2 3 4 5 6
	• Reflection on what the student learned about self as a learner is apparent.	0 1 2 3 4 5 6

Technological Products

Comments

_____

_____

Meaning of Performance Scale:

6—PROFESSIONAL LEVEL: level expected from a professional in the content area

5—ADVANCED LEVEL: level exceeds expectations of the standard

4—PROFICIENT LEVEL: level expected for meeting the standard

3—PROGRESSING LEVEL: level demonstrates movement toward the standard

2—NOVICE LEVEL: level demonstrates initial awareness and knowledge of standard

1—NONPERFORMING LEVEL: level indicates no effort made to meet standard

0—NONPARTICIPATING LEVEL: level indicates nothing turned in

COMPUTER GRAPHIC Tier 3—DAP TOOL

CONTENT	▪ Content is accurate and thorough in detail.	0 1 2 3 4 5 6
	▪ Product shows complex understanding and manipulation of content.	0 1 2 3 4 5 6
	▪ Product shows deep probing of content.	0 1 2 3 4 5 6
	▪ Organization is best suited to the product.	0 1 2 3 4 5 6
PRESENTATION		
CONCEPT	▪ The graphic employs a new idea. This is evident to the viewer as he experiences emotions, thoughts, and/or feelings when viewing it. The graphic may be delivering a message or making an impact on others beyond the targeted audience.	0 1 2 3 4 5 6
ELEMENTS AND PRINCIPLES OF DESIGN	▪ Elements of design strengthen the message and product, especially line, shape, color, and value. Principles of design strengthen the graphic as well, especially proportion, balance, contrast, rhythm, and unity.	0 1 2 3 4 5 6
TECHNOLOGY	▪ A skillful and original manipulation of image editing tools has created a graphic image that strongly and effectively communicates its purpose. Professional graphics applications have been intentionally implemented in an artistic way.	0 1 2 3 4 5 6
CREATIVITY	▪ Individual insight is originally expressed in relation to the content.	0 1 2 3 4 5 6
	▪ Individual spark is originally expressed in relation to the presentation.	0 1 2 3 4 5 6
REFLECTION	▪ Insightful reflection on the learning of the content through product development is expressed.	0 1 2 3 4 5 6
	▪ Insightful reflection on what the student learned about self as a learner is expressed.	0 1 2 3 4 5 6

Comments

_____

_____

Meaning of Performance Scale:

6—PROFESSIONAL LEVEL: level expected from a professional in the content area

5—ADVANCED LEVEL: level exceeds expectations of the standard

4—PROFICIENT LEVEL: level expected for meeting the standard

3—PROGRESSING LEVEL: level demonstrates movement toward the standard

2—NOVICE LEVEL: level demonstrates initial awareness and knowledge of standard

1—NONPERFORMING LEVEL: level indicates no effort made to meet standard

0—NONPARTICIPATING LEVEL: level indicates nothing turned in

COMPUTER PROGRAM Tier 1—DAP TOOL

CONTENT	▪ Is the content correct and complete?	0 1 2 3 4 5 6
	▪ Has the content been thought about in a way that goes beyond a surface understanding?	0 1 2 3 4 5 6
	▪ Is the content put together in such a way that people understand it?	0 1 2 3 4 5 6
PRESENTATION		
PROVISIONS	▪ Does the program address a real-world problem? Are the problem and solution correctly defined? Is the solution mapped well? Is the appropriate computer language used? Has the code been designed, implemented, and tested?	0 1 2 3 4 5 6
READABILITY	▪ Is the code well organized, easy to follow, and well documented? Does it demonstrate an understanding of syntax, semantics, control structures, and data representations? Are symbolic names easy to understand?	0 1 2 3 4 5 6
EFFICIENCY	▪ Is the program's length only as long as necessary? Is it efficient in its system resource consumption? Is the solution efficient?	0 1 2 3 4 5 6
RELIABILITY/ ROBUSTNESS	▪ Are the results correct? Are there very few errors? Does the code anticipate (and solve) conflicts with data? Does it address how a user handles error messages?	0 1 2 3 4 5 6
REUSABILITY/ PORTABILITY	▪ Can the code be reused in part or as a whole? Can it work in other software and hardware environments with very little reprogramming?	0 1 2 3 4 5 6
DOCUMENTATION	▪ Does the documentation clearly explain what the program does, why it does it the way it does, and how to use it? Has the proper technical format and appropriate grammar been used?	0 1 2 3 4 5 6
CREATIVITY	▪ Is the content seen in a new way?	0 1 2 3 4 5 6
	▪ Is the presentation done in a new way?	0 1 2 3 4 5 6
REFLECTION	▪ What did you learn about the content as you completed this product?	0 1 2 3 4 5 6
	▪ What did you learn about yourself as a learner by creating this product?	0 1 2 3 4 5 6

Technological Products

Comments _____

_____

Meaning of Performance Scale:

6—PROFESSIONAL LEVEL: level expected from a professional in the content area

5—ADVANCED LEVEL: level exceeds expectations of the standard

4—PROFICIENT LEVEL: level expected for meeting the standard

3—PROGRESSING LEVEL: level demonstrates movement toward the standard

2—NOVICE LEVEL: level demonstrates initial awareness and knowledge of standard

1—NONPERFORMING LEVEL: level indicates no effort made to meet standard

0—NONPARTICIPATING LEVEL: level indicates nothing turned in

COMPUTER PROGRAM Tier 2—DAP TOOL

CONTENT	▪ Content is accurate.	0 1 2 3 4 5 6
	▪ Content has depth and complexity of thought.	0 1 2 3 4 5 6
	▪ Content is organized.	0 1 2 3 4 5 6
PRESENTATION		
PROVISIONS	▪ Problem and solution are correctly and clearly defined with the solution mapped correctly. An appropriate computer language is used. Code has been designed, implemented, and tested well.	0 1 2 3 4 5 6
READABILITY	▪ Code is well organized, clear, and well documented. It demonstrates a clear understanding of syntax, semantics, control structures, and data representations. Symbolic names are readily understandable. The purpose is clearly explained.	0 1 2 3 4 5 6
EFFICIENCY	▪ The code is efficient and effective. System resource consumption is low. The solution is more efficient than other solutions considered.	0 1 2 3 4 5 6
RELIABILITY/ ROBUSTNESS	▪ Program analyzes data input for potential errors, illegal values, and other incompatibilities and notifies user. Error messages are concise, yet descriptive enough to properly identify the issue to the end user.	0 1 2 3 4 5 6
REUSABILITY/ PORTABILITY	▪ Code can easily be reused in part or as a whole. It can be compiled for use in different operating systems.	0 1 2 3 4 5 6
DOCUMENTATION	▪ Documentation clearly explains the functions of the program, the reasoning behind it, and how the functions are accomplished. All variables, input requirements, and output results are described. Proper technical format and appropriate grammar and usage have been used.	0 1 2 3 4 5 6
CREATIVITY	▪ Individual insight is expressed in relation to the content.	0 1 2 3 4 5 6
	▪ Individual spark is expressed in relation to the presentation.	0 1 2 3 4 5 6
REFLECTION	▪ Reflection on the learning of the content through product development is apparent.	0 1 2 3 4 5 6
	▪ Reflection on what the student learned about self as a learner is apparent.	0 1 2 3 4 5 6

Technological Products

Comments

_____

_____

Meaning of Performance Scale:

6—PROFESSIONAL LEVEL: level expected from a professional in the content area

5—ADVANCED LEVEL: level exceeds expectations of the standard

4—PROFICIENT LEVEL: level expected for meeting the standard

3—PROGRESSING LEVEL: level demonstrates movement toward the standard

2—NOVICE LEVEL: level demonstrates initial awareness and knowledge of standard

1—NONPERFORMING LEVEL: level indicates no effort made to meet standard

0—NONPARTICIPATING LEVEL: level indicates nothing turned in

COMPUTER PROGRAM Tier 3—DAP TOOL

CONTENT	• Content is accurate and thorough in detail.	0 1 2 3 4 5 6
	• Product shows complex understanding and manipulation of content.	0 1 2 3 4 5 6
	• Product shows deep probing of content.	0 1 2 3 4 5 6
	• Organization is best suited to the product.	0 1 2 3 4 5 6
PRESENTATION		
PROVISIONS	• Problem and solution are accurately and thoroughly defined with the solution mapped in the most efficient way. Computer language used is best suited for the problem. Code has been thoroughly designed, implemented, and tested.	0 1 2 3 4 5 6
READABILITY	• Code is exceptionally clear in its organization, simple to follow, and well documented. It demonstrates a strong manipulation of syntax, semantics, control structures, and data representations. Symbolic names and comments all support and clarify the purpose.	0 1 2 3 4 5 6
EFFICIENCY	• The code is highly efficient and effective. System resource consumption is the lowest possible. The solution is the most efficient from all those considered.	0 1 2 3 4 5 6
RELIABILITY/ ROBUSTNESS	• Program analyzes data input for potential errors, illegal values, and other incompatibilities and prompts user for corrections at time of entry. Error messages suggest possible solutions to user. Minimum systems requirements to run the program are fully identified.	0 1 2 3 4 5 6
REUSABILITY/ PORTABILITY	• Code can easily and efficiently be reused in part or in whole. It can be easily compiled for use in different operating systems.	0 1 2 3 4 5 6
DOCUMENTATION	• Using ideal technical format and appropriate grammar, documentation completely and concisely explains the functions of the program, the reasoning behind it, and how the functions are accomplished. All variables, input requirements, and output results are fully described.	0 1 2 3 4 5 6
CREATIVITY	• Individual insight is originally expressed in relation to the content.	0 1 2 3 4 5 6
	• Individual spark is originally expressed in relation to the presentation.	0 1 2 3 4 5 6
REFLECTION	• Insightful reflection on the learning of the content through product development is expressed.	0 1 2 3 4 5 6
	• Insightful reflection on what the student learned about self as a learner is expressed.	0 1 2 3 4 5 6

Technological Products

Comments

_____

_____

Meaning of Performance Scale:

6—PROFESSIONAL LEVEL: level expected from a professional in the content area

5—ADVANCED LEVEL: level exceeds expectations of the standard

4—PROFICIENT LEVEL: level expected for meeting the standard

3—PROGRESSING LEVEL: level demonstrates movement toward the standard

2—NOVICE LEVEL: level demonstrates initial awareness and knowledge of standard

1—NONPERFORMING LEVEL: level indicates no effort made to meet standard

0—NONPARTICIPATING LEVEL: level indicates nothing turned in

DOCUMENTARY Tier 1—DAP TOOL

CONTENT	▪ Is the content correct and complete?	0 1 2 3 4 5 6
	▪ Has the content been thought about in a way that goes beyond a surface understanding?	0 1 2 3 4 5 6
	▪ Is the content put together in such a way that people understand it?	0 1 2 3 4 5 6
PRESENTATION		
SCRIPT	▪ Does the script fully develop the purpose and theme? Is it persuasive? Is the narration or dialogue natural and important to the purpose? Is the title clear? Are credits listed?	0 1 2 3 4 5 6
AUDIO	▪ Does the narration help explain the main ideas or provide important information? Is the background music well suited to the topic? Do the audio elements develop the purpose and theme? Is the audio clear?	0 1 2 3 4 5 6
VISUAL	▪ Do the visual images match the script and add to the meaning? Are the transitions smooth from one image or clip to the next?	0 1 2 3 4 5 6
FILMING	▪ Is there control over the images? If a camera is used, do the camera angles vary? Is the movement from one image or one clip to the next purposeful? If special effects are used, do they add to the documentary?	0 1 2 3 4 5 6
CREATIVITY	▪ Is the content seen in a new way?	0 1 2 3 4 5 6
	▪ Is the presentation done in a new way?	0 1 2 3 4 5 6
REFLECTION	▪ What did you learn about the content as you completed this product?	0 1 2 3 4 5 6
	▪ What did you learn about yourself as a learner by creating this product?	0 1 2 3 4 5 6

Comments

Meaning of Performance Scale:

6—PROFESSIONAL LEVEL: level expected from a professional in the content area

5—ADVANCED LEVEL: level exceeds expectations of the standard

4—PROFICIENT LEVEL: level expected for meeting the standard

3—PROGRESSING LEVEL: level demonstrates movement toward the standard

2—NOVICE LEVEL: level demonstrates initial awareness and knowledge of standard

1—NONPERFORMING LEVEL: level indicates no effort made to meet standard

0—NONPARTICIPATING LEVEL: level indicates nothing turned in

Assessing Differentiated Student Products © Prufrock Press • This page may be photocopied or reproduced with permission for classroom use.

DOCUMENTARY Tier 2—DAP TOOL

CONTENT		
	▪ Content is accurate.	0 1 2 3 4 5 6
	▪ Content has depth and complexity of thought.	0 1 2 3 4 5 6
	▪ Content is organized.	0 1 2 3 4 5 6
PRESENTATION		
SCRIPT	▪ The script, fully developing purpose and theme, persuades the audience. Dialogue or narration is realistic. Title enhances the purpose.	0 1 2 3 4 5 6
AUDIO	▪ The narration skillfully develops the theme and purpose. All audio elements, including background music, intentionally develop essential elements. They are clear and free from distortion. Level of audio is appropriate.	0 1 2 3 4 5 6
VISUAL	▪ Images are appropriate and aid the audience's understanding and engagement. Scene transitions between images or movie clips are smooth and purposeful.	0 1 2 3 4 5 6
FILMING	▪ Camera angles and movement (or still images and movie clip selections) are intentional and help purpose. Special effects enhance the documentary.	0 1 2 3 4 5 6
CREATIVITY	▪ Individual insight is expressed in relation to the content.	0 1 2 3 4 5 6
	▪ Individual spark is expressed in relation to the presentation.	0 1 2 3 4 5 6
REFLECTION	▪ Reflection on the learning of the content through product development is apparent.	0 1 2 3 4 5 6
	▪ Reflection on what the student learned about self as a learner is apparent.	0 1 2 3 4 5 6

Comments

_____

_____

Meaning of Performance Scale:

6—PROFESSIONAL LEVEL: level expected from a professional in the content area

5—ADVANCED LEVEL: level exceeds expectations of the standard

4—PROFICIENT LEVEL: level expected for meeting the standard

3—PROGRESSING LEVEL: level demonstrates movement toward the standard

2—NOVICE LEVEL: level demonstrates initial awareness and knowledge of standard

1—NONPERFORMING LEVEL: level indicates no effort made to meet standard

0—NONPARTICIPATING LEVEL: level indicates nothing turned in

Documentary Tier 3—DAP TOOL

CONTENT	• Content is accurate and thorough in detail.	0 1 2 3 4 5 6
	• Product shows complex understanding and manipulation of content.	0 1 2 3 4 5 6
	• Product shows deep probing of content.	0 1 2 3 4 5 6
	• Organization is best suited to the product.	0 1 2 3 4 5 6
PRESENTATION		
SCRIPT	• The highly persuasive script skillfully develops purpose and theme. Dialogue or narration is insightful. A powerful message is delivered. Title reflects purpose.	0 1 2 3 4 5 6
AUDIO	• The narration proves critical to the intent and design of the documentary. The background music purposely enhances the essential elements. All audio elements are well controlled, free from distortion, and critical to purpose and theme.	0 1 2 3 4 5 6
VISUAL	• Images, whether still or moving, are engaging and original plus they enhance meaning. Transitions are seamless.	0 1 2 3 4 5 6
FILMING	• Intentional camera angles and movement (or intentional still images and movie clip selections) intensify the meaning. Special effects clarify and enhance purpose and theme.	0 1 2 3 4 5 6
CREATIVITY	• Individual insight is originally expressed in relation to the content.	0 1 2 3 4 5 6
	• Individual spark is originally expressed in relation to the presentation.	0 1 2 3 4 5 6
REFLECTION	• Insightful reflection on the learning of the content through product development is expressed.	0 1 2 3 4 5 6
	• Insightful reflection on what the student learned about self as a learner is expressed.	0 1 2 3 4 5 6

Technological Products

Comments

_____

_____

Meaning of Performance Scale:

6—PROFESSIONAL LEVEL: level expected from a professional in the content area

5—ADVANCED LEVEL: level exceeds expectations of the standard

4—PROFICIENT LEVEL: level expected for meeting the standard

3—PROGRESSING LEVEL: level demonstrates movement toward the standard

2—NOVICE LEVEL: level demonstrates initial awareness and knowledge of standard

1—NONPERFORMING LEVEL: level indicates no effort made to meet standard

0—NONPARTICIPATING LEVEL: level indicates nothing turned in

MOVIE Tier 1—DAP TOOL

CONTENT	▪ Is the content correct and complete?	0 1 2 3 4 5 6
	▪ Has the content been thought about in a way that goes beyond a surface understanding?	0 1 2 3 4 5 6
	▪ Is the content put together in such a way that people understand it?	0 1 2 3 4 5 6
PRESENTATION		
SCRIPT	▪ Does the script fully develop the purpose and theme? Is the dialogue natural to the character and important to the purpose? Is the title clear? Are credits listed?	0 1 2 3 4 5 6
AUDIO	▪ Does the narration help explain the main ideas or provide important information? Is the background music well suited to the topic? Do the audio elements develop the purpose and theme? Is the audio clear?	0 1 2 3 4 5 6
VISUAL	▪ Do the visual images match the script and add to the meaning? Are the transitions smooth from one image to the next or one clip to the next?	0 1 2 3 4 5 6
FILMING	▪ Is there control over the images? If a camera is used, do the camera angles vary? Is the movement from one image to the next or one clip to the next purposeful? If special effects are used, do they add to the movie?	0 1 2 3 4 5 6
CREATIVITY	▪ Is the content seen in a new way?	0 1 2 3 4 5 6
	▪ Is the presentation done in a new way?	0 1 2 3 4 5 6
REFLECTION	▪ What did you learn about the content as you completed this product?	0 1 2 3 4 5 6
	▪ What did you learn about yourself as a learner by creating this product?	0 1 2 3 4 5 6

Comments

_____

_____

Meaning of Performance Scale:

6—PROFESSIONAL LEVEL: level expected from a professional in the content area

5—ADVANCED LEVEL: level exceeds expectations of the standard

4—PROFICIENT LEVEL: level expected for meeting the standard

3—PROGRESSING LEVEL: level demonstrates movement toward the standard

2—NOVICE LEVEL: level demonstrates initial awareness and knowledge of standard

1—NONPERFORMING LEVEL: level indicates no effort made to meet standard

0—NONPARTICIPATING LEVEL: level indicates nothing turned in

MOVIE Tier 2—DAP TOOL

CONTENT	▪ Content is accurate.	0 1 2 3 4 5 6
	▪ Content has depth and complexity of thought.	0 1 2 3 4 5 6
	▪ Content is organized.	0 1 2 3 4 5 6
PRESENTATION		
SCRIPT	▪ The script fully develops purpose, theme, and plot/message. Dialogue is realistic to the character and aids in character development. Title enhances the purpose.	0 1 2 3 4 5 6
AUDIO	▪ The narration skillfully develops the theme and plot. All audio elements, including background music, intentionally develop essential elements. They are clear and free from distortion. The level of audio is appropriate.	0 1 2 3 4 5 6
VISUAL	▪ Images are appropriate and aid the audience's understanding and engagement. Scene transitions between images or movie clips are smooth and purposeful.	0 1 2 3 4 5 6
FILMING	▪ Camera angles and movement (or still images and movie clip selections) are purposeful and help develop characters and plot/message. Special effects enhance the movie.	0 1 2 3 4 5 6
CREATIVITY	▪ Individual insight is expressed in relation to the content.	0 1 2 3 4 5 6
	▪ Individual spark is expressed in relation to the presentation.	0 1 2 3 4 5 6
REFLECTION	▪ Reflection on the learning of the content through product development is apparent.	0 1 2 3 4 5 6
	▪ Reflection on what the student learned about self as a learner is apparent.	0 1 2 3 4 5 6

Comments

_____

_____

Meaning of Performance Scale:

6—PROFESSIONAL LEVEL: level expected from a professional in the content area

5—ADVANCED LEVEL: level exceeds expectations of the standard

4—PROFICIENT LEVEL: level expected for meeting the standard

3—PROGRESSING LEVEL: level demonstrates movement toward the standard

2—NOVICE LEVEL: level demonstrates initial awareness and knowledge of standard

1—NONPERFORMING LEVEL: level indicates no effort made to meet standard

0—NONPARTICIPATING LEVEL: level indicates nothing turned in

MOVIE Tier 3—DAP TOOL

CONTENT	• Content is accurate and thorough in detail.	0 1 2 3 4 5 6
	• Product shows complex understanding and manipulation of content.	0 1 2 3 4 5 6
	• Product shows deep probing of content.	0 1 2 3 4 5 6
	• Organization is best suited to the product.	0 1 2 3 4 5 6
PRESENTATION		
SCRIPT	• Script skillfully develops plot/message, character, purpose, and theme. Dialogue is insightful and develops the character. A powerful message is delivered. Title reflects purpose.	0 1 2 3 4 5 6
AUDIO	• The narration proves critical to the intent and design of the movie. The background music purposefully enhances the essential elements. All audio elements are well controlled, free from distortion, and critical to purpose and theme.	0 1 2 3 4 5 6
VISUAL	• Images are engaging and original, plus they enhance meaning. Transitions are seamless. Images, whether still or moving, are engaging and original, and they enhance meaning.	0 1 2 3 4 5 6
FILMING	• Special effects clarify and enhance purpose and theme. Intentional camera angles and movement (or intentional still images and movie clip selections) intensify the meaning.	0 1 2 3 4 5 6
CREATIVITY	• Individual insight is originally expressed in relation to the content.	0 1 2 3 4 5 6
	• Individual spark is originally expressed in relation to the presentation.	0 1 2 3 4 5 6
REFLECTION	• Insightful reflection on the learning of the content through product development is expressed.	0 1 2 3 4 5 6
	• Insightful reflection on what the student learned about self as a learner is expressed.	0 1 2 3 4 5 6

Comments

_____

Meaning of Performance Scale:

6—PROFESSIONAL LEVEL: level expected from a professional in the content area

5—ADVANCED LEVEL: level exceeds expectations of the standard

4—PROFICIENT LEVEL: level expected for meeting the standard

3—PROGRESSING LEVEL: level demonstrates movement toward the standard

2—NOVICE LEVEL: level demonstrates initial awareness and knowledge of standard

1—NONPERFORMING LEVEL: level indicates no effort made to meet standard

0—NONPARTICIPATING LEVEL: level indicates nothing turned in

PODCAST Tier 1—DAP TOOL

CONTENT	▪ Is the content correct and complete?	0 1 2 3 4 5 6
	▪ Has the content been thought about in a way that goes beyond a surface understanding?	0 1 2 3 4 5 6
	▪ Is the content put together in such a way that people understand it?	0 1 2 3 4 5 6
PRESENTATION		
RELEVANCE OF CONTENT	▪ Does the content relate to the purpose? Is the content designed for a real-world audience? Are the resources valid, reliable, and recent?	0 1 2 3 4 5 6
DELIVERY	▪ Are the voices clear and articulate? Are the speaker(s), date, location, and topic introduced? Does the speaker(s) engage the audience and maintain its interest? Does it flow well?	0 1 2 3 4 5 6
ENHANCEMENTS	▪ Do all graphics (e.g., photos, music, text, video) relate to the purpose? Are they interesting, of good quality, and smoothly incorporated? Are all copyright guidelines followed? Is the cover art attractive?	0 1 2 3 4 5 6
TECHNICAL PRODUCTION	▪ Is the audio strong, free from unwanted noise with a consistent level? Is the length appropriate for the topic and the audience? Is the podcast linked from a site that includes subject tags and other links? Is it available in various file formats? Is a written transcript available? Are metadata complete?	0 1 2 3 4 5 6
CREATIVITY	▪ Is the content seen in a new way?	0 1 2 3 4 5 6
	▪ Is the presentation done in a new way?	0 1 2 3 4 5 6
REFLECTION	▪ What did you learn about the content as you completed this product?	0 1 2 3 4 5 6
	▪ What did you learn about yourself as a learner by creating this product?	0 1 2 3 4 5 6

Technological Products

Comments

_____

_____

Meaning of Performance Scale:

6—PROFESSIONAL LEVEL: level expected from a professional in the content area

5—ADVANCED LEVEL: level exceeds expectations of the standard

4—PROFICIENT LEVEL: level expected for meeting the standard

3—PROGRESSING LEVEL: level demonstrates movement toward the standard

2—NOVICE LEVEL: level demonstrates initial awareness and knowledge of standard

1—NONPERFORMING LEVEL: level indicates no effort made to meet standard

0—NONPARTICIPATING LEVEL: level indicates nothing turned in

PODCAST Tier 2—DAP TOOL

CONTENT	▪ Content is accurate.	0 1 2 3 4 5 6
	▪ Content has depth and complexity of thought.	0 1 2 3 4 5 6
	▪ Content is organized.	0 1 2 3 4 5 6
PRESENTATION		
RELEVANCE OF CONTENT	▪ The content directly supports the purpose. All material is highly appropriate for the intended audience. Resources contain up-to-date, valid, and pertinent information.	0 1 2 3 4 5 6
DELIVERY	▪ Voice is strong and clear with appropriate intonations. Speaker(s) stirs interest in the audience. Introduction clearly establishes speaker(s), date, place, and topic. Podcast flows naturally.	0 1 2 3 4 5 6
ENHANCEMENTS	▪ All graphics (e.g., photos, music, text, video) relate directly to the purpose, create interest, and are of very high quality. Both audio and video enhance the pages with appropriate sound level, quality, and purpose. Copyright guidelines are followed. Cover art engages the audience.	0 1 2 3 4 5 6
TECHNICAL PRODUCTION	▪ Audio is strong, clear, consistent, and free from unwanted noise. Video resolution is acceptable when viewed at a variety of screen sizes. Length, while appropriate for topic, maintains audience's interest. Podcast is linked from a site that includes subject tags and other links. It is readily available in various file formats. A written transcript also is readily available. Metadata allow the audience to find the podcast easily.	0 1 2 3 4 5 6
CREATIVITY	▪ Individual insight is expressed in relation to the content.	0 1 2 3 4 5 6
	▪ Individual spark is expressed in relation to the presentation.	0 1 2 3 4 5 6
REFLECTION	▪ Reflection on the learning of the content through product development is apparent.	0 1 2 3 4 5 6
	▪ Reflection on what the student learned about self as a learner is apparent.	0 1 2 3 4 5 6

Technological Products

Comments

_____

_____

Meaning of Performance Scale:

6—PROFESSIONAL LEVEL: level expected from a professional in the content area

5—ADVANCED LEVEL: level exceeds expectations of the standard

4—PROFICIENT LEVEL: level expected for meeting the standard

3—PROGRESSING LEVEL: level demonstrates movement toward the standard

2—NOVICE LEVEL: level demonstrates initial awareness and knowledge of standard

1—NONPERFORMING LEVEL: level indicates no effort made to meet standard

0—NONPARTICIPATING LEVEL: level indicates nothing turned in

PODCAST Tier 3—DAP TOOL

CONTENT	▪ Content is accurate and thorough in detail.	0 1 2 3 4 5 6
	▪ Product shows complex understanding and manipulation of content.	0 1 2 3 4 5 6
	▪ Product shows deep probing of content.	0 1 2 3 4 5 6
	▪ Organization is best suited to the product.	0 1 2 3 4 5 6
PRESENTATION		
RELEVANCE OF CONTENT	▪ All content strongly supports and develops the purpose. High-quality resources further develop the purpose by containing relevant, current, and valid information. Everything fully relates to the target audience.	0 1 2 3 4 5 6
DELIVERY	▪ The voice is strong, clear, and effective with ideal intonations and volume. Speaker engages audience and exudes enthusiasm. A complete introduction clearly establishes speaker(s), date, place, and topic. Elements blend together seamlessly.	0 1 2 3 4 5 6
ENHANCEMENTS	▪ All graphics (e.g., photos, music, text, video) enhance the purpose, create and maintain interest, and are of exceptional quality. All audio and video incorporated is artfully done, ensuring optimum sound level, quality, and purpose. Copyright guidelines are strictly followed. Engaging cover art piques interest.	0 1 2 3 4 5 6
TECHNICAL PRODUCTION	▪ Audio successfully filters unwanted noise. Consistent and clear, the audio level enhances the production. Video is high resolution and sharp when viewed at a variety of sizes. Length engages audience. Available in multiple file formats, podcast is clearly linked from a site that includes descriptive subject tags and other pertinent links. A written transcript is easy to find. Robust metadata dictate that the podcast can be easily found in many ways.	0 1 2 3 4 5 6
CREATIVITY	▪ Individual insight is originally expressed in relation to the content.	0 1 2 3 4 5 6
	▪ Individual spark is originally expressed in relation to the presentation.	0 1 2 3 4 5 6
REFLECTION	▪ Insightful reflection on the learning of the content through product development is expressed.	0 1 2 3 4 5 6
	▪ Insightful reflection on what the student learned about self as a learner is expressed.	0 1 2 3 4 5 6

Comments

_____

_____

Meaning of Performance Scale:

6—PROFESSIONAL LEVEL: level expected from a professional in the content area

5—ADVANCED LEVEL: level exceeds expectations of the standard

4—PROFICIENT LEVEL: level expected for meeting the standard

3—PROGRESSING LEVEL: level demonstrates movement toward the standard

2—NOVICE LEVEL: level demonstrates initial awareness and knowledge of standard

1—NONPERFORMING LEVEL: level indicates no effort made to meet standard

0—NONPARTICIPATING LEVEL: level indicates nothing turned in

POWERPOINT Tier 1—DAP TOOL

CONTENT		
	▪ Is the content correct and complete?	0 1 2 3 4 5 6
	▪ Has the content been thought about in a way that goes beyond a surface understanding?	0 1 2 3 4 5 6
	▪ Is the content put together in such a way that people understand it?	0 1 2 3 4 5 6
PRESENTATION		
TEXT	▪ Is the title clear? Does the text explain the topic without too much information on any one slide?	0 1 2 3 4 5 6
GRAPHICS	▪ Are the graphics (illustrations, photos, videos) important to the topic? Is there a careful mixture of text and graphics?	0 1 2 3 4 5 6
SLIDES	▪ Do the slides make sense following one another in both how they look and in what they mean? Does the slideshow appeal to the audience? Does it have appropriate transitions?	0 1 2 3 4 5 6
CREATIVITY	▪ Is the content seen in a new way?	0 1 2 3 4 5 6
	▪ Is the presentation done in a new way?	0 1 2 3 4 5 6
REFLECTION	▪ What did you learn about the content as you completed this product?	0 1 2 3 4 5 6
	▪ What did you learn about yourself as a learner by creating this product?	0 1 2 3 4 5 6

Technological Products

Comments

_____

_____

Meaning of Performance Scale:

6—PROFESSIONAL LEVEL: level expected from a professional in the content area

5—ADVANCED LEVEL: level exceeds expectations of the standard

4—PROFICIENT LEVEL: level expected for meeting the standard

3—PROGRESSING LEVEL: level demonstrates movement toward the standard

2—NOVICE LEVEL: level demonstrates initial awareness and knowledge of standard

1—NONPERFORMING LEVEL: level indicates no effort made to meet standard

0—NONPARTICIPATING LEVEL: level indicates nothing turned in

Note. Adapted from *Strategies for Differentiating Instruction: Best Practices for the Classroom* (p. 202), by J. L. Roberts and T. F. Inman, 2007, Waco, TX: Prufrock Press. Copyright © 2007 by Prufrock Press. Adapted with permission.

POWERPOINT Tier 2—DAP TOOL

CONTENT	• Content is accurate.	0 1 2 3 4 5 6
	• Content has depth and complexity of thought.	0 1 2 3 4 5 6
	• Content is organized.	0 1 2 3 4 5 6
PRESENTATION		
TEXT	• Title enhances the PowerPoint. Text highlights most important concepts in topic in clearly organized slides. Text is limited to key ideas.	0 1 2 3 4 5 6
GRAPHICS	• Graphics (illustrations, photos, videos) add information to the topic. Layout design is organized and attractive.	0 1 2 3 4 5 6
SLIDES	• Slides maintain continuity in form and purpose. Slideshow keeps audience's attention through graphics, text, and special effects.	0 1 2 3 4 5 6
CREATIVITY	• Individual insight is expressed in relation to the content.	0 1 2 3 4 5 6
	• Individual spark is expressed in relation to the presentation.	0 1 2 3 4 5 6
REFLECTION	• Reflection on the learning of the content through product development is apparent.	0 1 2 3 4 5 6
	• Reflection on what the student learned about self as a learner is apparent.	0 1 2 3 4 5 6

Comments

_____

_____

Meaning of Performance Scale:

6—PROFESSIONAL LEVEL: level expected from a professional in the content area

5—ADVANCED LEVEL: level exceeds expectations of the standard

4—PROFICIENT LEVEL: level expected for meeting the standard

3—PROGRESSING LEVEL: level demonstrates movement toward the standard

2—NOVICE LEVEL: level demonstrates initial awareness and knowledge of standard

1—NONPERFORMING LEVEL: level indicates no effort made to meet standard

0—NONPARTICIPATING LEVEL: level indicates nothing turned in

Note. Adapted from *Strategies for Differentiating Instruction: Best Practices for the Classroom* (p. 203), by J. L. Roberts and T. F. Inman, 2007, Waco, TX: Prufrock Press. Copyright © 2007 by Prufrock Press. Adapted with permission.

POWERPOINT Tier 3—DAP TOOL

CONTENT	· Content is accurate and thorough in detail.	0 1 2 3 4 5 6
	· Product shows complex understanding and manipulation of content.	0 1 2 3 4 5 6
	· Product shows deep probing of content.	0 1 2 3 4 5 6
	· Organization is best suited to the product.	0 1 2 3 4 5 6
PRESENTATION		
TEXT	· Title reflects purpose. Text highlights most important concepts in clear, concise manner with careful thought given to amount and type of information on each slide.	0 1 2 3 4 5 6
GRAPHICS	· Graphics (illustrations, photos, videos) enhance meaning. Thoughtful manipulation of color, layout, and font reflects purpose.	0 1 2 3 4 5 6
SLIDES	· The continuity of the slides (font, color, background, movement, sound, and special effects) enhances the meaning. Slideshow engages the audience through its graphics, text, appearance, movement, sounds, and special effects.	0 1 2 3 4 5 6
CREATIVITY	· Individual insight is originally expressed in relation to the content.	0 1 2 3 4 5 6
	· Individual spark is originally expressed in relation to the presentation.	0 1 2 3 4 5 6
REFLECTION	· Insightful reflection on the learning of the content through product development is expressed.	0 1 2 3 4 5 6
	· Insightful reflection on what the student learned about self as a learner is expressed.	0 1 2 3 4 5 6

Comments

_____

_____

Meaning of Performance Scale:

6—PROFESSIONAL LEVEL: level expected from a professional in the content area

5—ADVANCED LEVEL: level exceeds expectations of the standard

4—PROFICIENT LEVEL: level expected for meeting the standard

3—PROGRESSING LEVEL: level demonstrates movement toward the standard

2—NOVICE LEVEL: level demonstrates initial awareness and knowledge of standard

1—NONPERFORMING LEVEL: level indicates no effort made to meet standard

0—NONPARTICIPATING LEVEL: level indicates nothing turned in

Note. Adapted from *Strategies for Differentiating Instruction: Best Practices for the Classroom* (p. 204), by J. L. Roberts and T. F. Inman, 2007, Waco, TX: Prufrock Press. Copyright © 2007 by Prufrock Press. Adapted with permission.

WEB PAGE Tier 1—DAP TOOL

CONTENT	▪ Is the content correct and complete?	0 1 2 3 4 5 6
	▪ Has the content been thought about in a way that goes beyond a surface understanding?	0 1 2 3 4 5 6
	▪ Is the content put together in such a way that people understand it?	0 1 2 3 4 5 6
PRESENTATION		
RELEVANCE OF CONTENT	▪ Does all of the content relate to the purpose? Is the content appropriate for the audience? Is the content useful? Are the resources valid, reliable, and recent? Do the outside links contain worthwhile, appropriate information related to the purpose?	0 1 2 3 4 5 6
STRUCTURE AND NAVIGATION	▪ Are all links, buttons, menus, and internal and external links clearly marked and properly labeled? Do they take the user to the appropriate place? Do the pages and paths flow logically? Does every menu and link connect to the home page? Is a site map or index provided?	0 1 2 3 4 5 6
TEXT, GRAPHICS, AND LAYOUT	▪ Is the font easy to read and appropriate for the various headings and sections? Does the use of italics, bold, and bullets make the page easier to understand and navigate? Do all graphics (e.g., photos, sound, video, animation) relate to the purpose? Are they interesting and of good quality? Are the backgrounds, colors, and use of white space pleasing to the eye? Are the text, graphics, and layout consistent across pages? Is the audio appropriate? Is the contact, copyright, and update information listed? Is the page ADA compliant? Are all sources cited correctly? Has the page been designed to work well on both Macs and PCs?	0 1 2 3 4 5 6
CREATIVITY	▪ Is the content seen in a new way?	0 1 2 3 4 5 6
	▪ Is the presentation done in a new way?	0 1 2 3 4 5 6
REFLECTION	▪ What did you learn about the content as you completed this product?	0 1 2 3 4 5 6
	▪ What did you learn about yourself as a learner by creating this product?	0 1 2 3 4 5 6

Comments

Meaning of Performance Scale:

6—PROFESSIONAL LEVEL: level expected from a professional in the content area

5—ADVANCED LEVEL: level exceeds expectations of the standard

4—PROFICIENT LEVEL: level expected for meeting the standard

3—PROGRESSING LEVEL: level demonstrates movement toward the standard

2—NOVICE LEVEL: level demonstrates initial awareness and knowledge of standard

1—NONPERFORMING LEVEL: level indicates no effort made to meet standard

0—NONPARTICIPATING LEVEL: level indicates nothing turned in

WEB PAGE Tier 2—DAP TOOL

CONTENT		
	▪ Content is accurate.	0 1 2 3 4 5 6
	▪ Content has depth and complexity of thought.	0 1 2 3 4 5 6
	▪ Content is organized.	0 1 2 3 4 5 6

PRESENTATION		
RELEVANCE OF CONTENT	▪ The content directly supports the purpose. All material is highly appropriate for the intended audience. Resources within the page as well as outside links contain up-to-date, valid, and pertinent information.	0 1 2 3 4 5 6
STRUCTURE AND NAVIGATION	▪ All buttons, menus, internal links, and external links are appropriately labeled, logically identified, functioning, and load well. All lines work in a logical fashion. Pages and paths flow smoothly. All pages, menus, and links connect back to the home page. The site map or index organizes the page and encourages easy use.	0 1 2 3 4 5 6
TEXT, GRAPHICS, AND LAYOUT	▪ Font styles, colors, and sizes are pleasing to the eye, readable, and appropriate for the meaning of the text and purpose of the page. Careful use of indentations, italics, bold, and bullets strengthens the clarity of the text and aids in navigation. All graphics (e.g., photos, sound, animation, video) relate directly to the purpose, create interest, and are of very high quality. Careful attention has been paid to backgrounds, colors, vertical and horizontal white space, and markings for visited and unvisited sites so that the page is seen as an engaging, coherent whole. Both audio and video enhance the pages with appropriate sound level, quality, and purpose. Information for contacts, copyright, and updates is readily accessible. All sources used are relevant and cited correctly. The ADA compliant page works equally well for PCs and Macs.	0 1 2 3 4 5 6

CREATIVITY		
	▪ Individual insight is expressed in relation to the content.	0 1 2 3 4 5 6
	▪ Individual spark is expressed in relation to the presentation.	0 1 2 3 4 5 6

REFLECTION		
	▪ Reflection on the learning of the content through product development is apparent.	0 1 2 3 4 5 6
	▪ Reflection on what the student learned about self as a learner is apparent.	0 1 2 3 4 5 6

Technological Products

Comments

_____

_____

Meaning of Performance Scale:

6—PROFESSIONAL LEVEL: level expected from a professional in the content area

5—ADVANCED LEVEL: level exceeds expectations of the standard

4—PROFICIENT LEVEL: level expected for meeting the standard

3—PROGRESSING LEVEL: level demonstrates movement toward the standard

2—NOVICE LEVEL: level demonstrates initial awareness and knowledge of standard

1—NONPERFORMING LEVEL: level indicates no effort made to meet standard

0—NONPARTICIPATING LEVEL: level indicates nothing turned in

WEB PAGE Tier 3—DAP TOOL

CONTENT	▪ Content is accurate and thorough in detail.	0 1 2 3 4 5 6
	▪ Product shows complex understanding and manipulation of content.	0 1 2 3 4 5 6
	▪ Product shows deep probing of content.	0 1 2 3 4 5 6
	▪ Organization is best suited to the product.	0 1 2 3 4 5 6

PRESENTATION

RELEVANCE OF CONTENT	▪ All content strongly supports and develops the purpose. High-quality resources and outside links further develop the purpose by containing relevant, current, and valid information. Everything fully relates to the target audience.	0 1 2 3 4 5 6
STRUCTURE AND NAVIGATION	▪ All buttons, menus, internal links, and external links are ideally labeled and identified, fully functioning, and load quickly. Logic governs the entire site, creating seamless navigation. All pages, menus, and links connect to the home page. The site map or index serves as an organizer, allowing users to find items quickly and easily.	0 1 2 3 4 5 6
TEXT, GRAPHICS, AND LAYOUT	▪ Font styles, colors, and sizes are very attractive, easy to read, and highly appropriate for the meaning of the text and purpose of the page. Creative use of indentations, italics, bold, and bullets strengthens the clarity of the text and aids in navigation. All graphics (e.g., photos, sound, animation, video) enhance the purpose, create and maintain interest, and are of exceptional quality. Backgrounds, colors, vertical and horizontal white space, and markings for visited and unvisited sites have been artfully designed to create a coherent whole that is readily understood. All audio and video are artfully done, ensuring optimum sound level and quality. Pertinent information for contacts, copyright, and updates is clearly marked. Sources are insightful, enhance the purpose of the page, and are cited correctly. The ADA compliant page works beautifully for both PCs and Macs.	0 1 2 3 4 5 6

CREATIVITY	▪ Individual insight is originally expressed in relation to the content.	0 1 2 3 4 5 6
	▪ Individual spark is originally expressed in relation to the presentation.	0 1 2 3 4 5 6

REFLECTION	▪ Insightful reflection on the learning of the content through product development is expressed.	0 1 2 3 4 5 6
	▪ Insightful reflection on what the student learned about self as a learner is expressed.	0 1 2 3 4 5 6

Comments

_____

_____

Meaning of Performance Scale:

6—PROFESSIONAL LEVEL: level expected from a professional in the content area

5—ADVANCED LEVEL: level exceeds expectations of the standard

4—PROFICIENT LEVEL: level expected for meeting the standard

3—PROGRESSING LEVEL: level demonstrates movement toward the standard

2—NOVICE LEVEL: level demonstrates initial awareness and knowledge of standard

1—NONPERFORMING LEVEL: level indicates no effort made to meet standard

0—NONPARTICIPATING LEVEL: level indicates nothing turned in

CARTOON Tier 1—DAP TOOL

CONTENT	▪ Is the content correct and complete?	0 1 2 3 4 5 6
	▪ Has the content been thought about in a way that goes beyond a surface understanding?	0 1 2 3 4 5 6
	▪ Is the content put together in such a way that people understand it?	0 1 2 3 4 5 6
PRESENTATION		
PURPOSE	▪ Will the readers laugh or be amused?	0 1 2 3 4 5 6
ILLUSTRATION	▪ Is the illustration clear and easy to understand? Does the illustration help the reader appreciate the humor?	0 1 2 3 4 5 6
LAYOUT	▪ Is the cartoon a single cell or does it have multiple cells? Is it the best number to get across the purpose?	0 1 2 3 4 5 6
TEXT (OPTIONAL)	▪ Is the title clear? If used, are the character balloons easy to read? Is the text clear and to the point? Does it complement the illustration?	0 1 2 3 4 5 6
CREATIVITY	▪ Is the content seen in a new way?	0 1 2 3 4 5 6
	▪ Is the presentation done in a new way?	0 1 2 3 4 5 6
REFLECTION	▪ What did you learn about the content as you completed this product?	0 1 2 3 4 5 6
	▪ What did you learn about yourself as a learner by creating this product?	0 1 2 3 4 5 6

Comments

_____

_____

Meaning of Performance Scale:

6—PROFESSIONAL LEVEL: level expected from a professional in the content area

5—ADVANCED LEVEL: level exceeds expectations of the standard

4—PROFICIENT LEVEL: level expected for meeting the standard

3—PROGRESSING LEVEL: level demonstrates movement toward the standard

2—NOVICE LEVEL: level demonstrates initial awareness and knowledge of standard

1—NONPERFORMING LEVEL: level indicates no effort made to meet standard

0—NONPARTICIPATING LEVEL: level indicates nothing turned in

Visual Products

CARTOON Tier 2—DAP TOOL

CONTENT	• Content is accurate.	0 1 2 3 4 5 6
	• Content has depth and complexity of thought.	0 1 2 3 4 5 6
	• Content is organized.	0 1 2 3 4 5 6
PRESENTATION		
PURPOSE	• The cartoon is designed for a specific audience as evidenced in text, illustration, and layout. The intended audience will find humor or amusement in the cartoon.	0 1 2 3 4 5 6
ILLUSTRATION	• The illustration enhances or embodies the humor. It aids the reader's understanding and increases enjoyment.	0 1 2 3 4 5 6
LAYOUT	• Whether single- or multicelled, the layout enhances the enjoyment and understanding of the cartoon.	0 1 2 3 4 5 6
TEXT (OPTIONAL)	• Title enhances the cartoon. The text effectively complements the purpose. The text incorporates word play, allusions, or parody effectively. If used, character balloons are well incorporated.	0 1 2 3 4 5 6
CREATIVITY	• Individual insight is expressed in relation to the content.	0 1 2 3 4 5 6
	• Individual spark is expressed in relation to the presentation.	0 1 2 3 4 5 6
REFLECTION	• Reflection on the learning of the content through product development is apparent.	0 1 2 3 4 5 6
	• Reflection on what the student learned about self as a learner is apparent.	0 1 2 3 4 5 6

Comments

_____

_____

Meaning of Performance Scale:

6—PROFESSIONAL LEVEL: level expected from a professional in the content area

5—ADVANCED LEVEL: level exceeds expectations of the standard

4—PROFICIENT LEVEL: level expected for meeting the standard

3—PROGRESSING LEVEL: level demonstrates movement toward the standard

2—NOVICE LEVEL: level demonstrates initial awareness and knowledge of standard

1—NONPERFORMING LEVEL: level indicates no effort made to meet standard

0—NONPARTICIPATING LEVEL: level indicates nothing turned in

Visual Products

CARTOON Tier 3—DAP TOOL

CONTENT	▪ Content is accurate and thorough in detail.	0 1 2 3 4 5 6
	▪ Product shows complex understanding and manipulation of content.	0 1 2 3 4 5 6
	▪ Product shows deep probing of content.	0 1 2 3 4 5 6
	▪ Organization is best suited to the product.	0 1 2 3 4 5 6
PRESENTATION		
PURPOSE	▪ The cartoon is deliberately created for a specific contemporary audience. The text, illustration, and layout all fully support the specific viewpoint of the cartoonist in regard to a current event, person, or situation. Reader's rights are respected and honored.	0 1 2 3 4 5 6
ILLUSTRATION	▪ Humor and purpose, inherent in the illustration, play an integral role in the reader's appreciation.	0 1 2 3 4 5 6
LAYOUT	▪ The number of cells purposely supports and furthers the cartoon's meaning.	0 1 2 3 4 5 6
TEXT (OPTIONAL)	▪ Title reflects the purpose of the cartoon. The text fully complements and enhances the purpose. The text artfully incorporates word play, allusions, or parody to reflect the purpose. If used, character balloons enhance the overall meaning of the cartoon.	0 1 2 3 4 5 6
CREATIVITY	▪ Individual insight is originally expressed in relation to the content.	0 1 2 3 4 5 6
	▪ Individual spark is originally expressed in relation to the presentation.	0 1 2 3 4 5 6
REFLECTION	▪ Insightful reflection on the learning of the content through product development is expressed.	0 1 2 3 4 5 6
	▪ Insightful reflection on what the student learned about self as a learner is expressed.	0 1 2 3 4 5 6

Comments

_____

_____

Meaning of Performance Scale:

6—PROFESSIONAL LEVEL: level expected from a professional in the content area

5—ADVANCED LEVEL: level exceeds expectations of the standard

4—PROFICIENT LEVEL: level expected for meeting the standard

3—PROGRESSING LEVEL: level demonstrates movement toward the standard

2—NOVICE LEVEL: level demonstrates initial awareness and knowledge of standard

1—NONPERFORMING LEVEL: level indicates no effort made to meet standard

0—NONPARTICIPATING LEVEL: level indicates nothing turned in

Visual Products

COLLAGE Tier 1—DAP TOOL

CONTENT	▪ Is the content correct and complete?	0 1 2 3 4 5 6
	▪ Has the content been thought about in a way that goes beyond a surface understanding?	0 1 2 3 4 5 6
	▪ Is the content put together in such a way that people understand it?	0 1 2 3 4 5 6
PRESENTATION		
PURPOSE	▪ Is the purpose or message communicated clearly?	0 1 2 3 4 5 6
TEXT	▪ Is the title easy to see and understand? If used, do the captions clearly explain the graphics or in some way enhance the collage?	0 1 2 3 4 5 6
GRAPHICS	▪ Are the images relevant to the topic? Do they help the audience understand the message? Are ideas in the collage consistent with its message and topic? Are details included to support or explain the message?	0 1 2 3 4 5 6
LAYOUT	▪ Is the layout of the images successfully organized to enhance the visual communication? If used, is the labeling linked to the graphic? Is there a border? Do the graphics and text create a strong message in how they are presented? Does the layout of the graphics and text appeal to the viewer?	0 1 2 3 4 5 6
MATERIALS	▪ Are appropriate materials used?	0 1 2 3 4 5 6
ELEMENTS AND PRINCIPLES OF DESIGN	▪ How are the elements of design included, especially size, texture, and color? How are the principles of design included, especially emphasis, balance, and unity?	0 1 2 3 4 5 6
CREATIVITY	▪ Is the content seen in a new way?	0 1 2 3 4 5 6
	▪ Is the presentation done in a new way?	0 1 2 3 4 5 6
REFLECTION	▪ What did you learn about the content as you completed this product?	0 1 2 3 4 5 6
	▪ What did you learn about yourself as a learner by creating this product?	0 1 2 3 4 5 6

Comments

_____

_____

Meaning of Performance Scale:

6—PROFESSIONAL LEVEL: level expected from a professional in the content area

5—ADVANCED LEVEL: level exceeds expectations of the standard

4—PROFICIENT LEVEL: level expected for meeting the standard

3—PROGRESSING LEVEL: level demonstrates movement toward the standard

2—NOVICE LEVEL: level demonstrates initial awareness and knowledge of standard

1—NONPERFORMING LEVEL: level indicates no effort made to meet standard

0—NONPARTICIPATING LEVEL: level indicates nothing turned in

COLLAGE Tier 2—DAP TOOL

CONTENT	▪ Content is accurate.	0 1 2 3 4 5 6
	▪ Content has depth and complexity of thought.	0 1 2 3 4 5 6
	▪ Content is organized.	0 1 2 3 4 5 6
PRESENTATION		
PURPOSE	▪ Purpose or message is clearly evident in text, graphics, layout, and materials.	0 1 2 3 4 5 6
TEXT	▪ Title reflects the purpose. If used, captions strongly link to purpose and add to the visual impact.	0 1 2 3 4 5 6
GRAPHICS	▪ Graphics add information, are appropriate, and enhance understanding. Multiple details support the purpose. All graphics clearly link to the main idea.	0 1 2 3 4 5 6
LAYOUT	▪ Design clearly emphasizes the message in an organized, attractive manner. Intentional overlapping of elements enhances the meaning and artistic appeal. Text, if used, is placed to clearly support the message. Careful planning has been given to layout.	0 1 2 3 4 5 6
MATERIALS	▪ A variety of materials is utilized, all of which aid in developing the purpose.	0 1 2 3 4 5 6
ELEMENTS AND PRINCIPLES OF DESIGN	▪ Elements of design are effectively incorporated, especially line, shape, size, texture, and color. Principles of design are effectively incorporated, especially balance, repetition, contrast, harmony, emphasis, and unity.	0 1 2 3 4 5 6
CREATIVITY	▪ Individual insight is expressed in relation to the content.	0 1 2 3 4 5 6
	▪ Individual spark is expressed in relation to the presentation.	0 1 2 3 4 5 6
REFLECTION	▪ Reflection on the learning of the content through product development is apparent.	0 1 2 3 4 5 6
	▪ Reflection on what the student learned about self as a learner is apparent.	0 1 2 3 4 5 6

Visual Products

Comments

_____

_____

Meaning of Performance Scale:

6—PROFESSIONAL LEVEL: level expected from a professional in the content area

5—ADVANCED LEVEL: level exceeds expectations of the standard

4—PROFICIENT LEVEL: level expected for meeting the standard

3—PROGRESSING LEVEL: level demonstrates movement toward the standard

2—NOVICE LEVEL: level demonstrates initial awareness and knowledge of standard

1—NONPERFORMING LEVEL: level indicates no effort made to meet standard

0—NONPARTICIPATING LEVEL: level indicates nothing turned in

COLLAGE Tier 3—DAP TOOL

CONTENT	▪ Content is accurate and thorough in detail.	0 1 2 3 4 5 6
	▪ Product shows complex understanding and manipulation of content.	0 1 2 3 4 5 6
	▪ Product shows deep probing of content.	0 1 2 3 4 5 6
	▪ Organization is best suited to the product.	0 1 2 3 4 5 6
PRESENTATION		
PURPOSE	▪ Purpose or message is strategically presented through successful manipulation of text, graphics, layout, and materials.	0 1 2 3 4 5 6
TEXT	▪ Title and captions fully develop and integrate the purpose of the collage.	0 1 2 3 4 5 6
GRAPHICS	▪ Graphics strongly enhance meaning, aid in understanding, and are best suited for the purpose. Elaborate details fully develop and integrate the purpose of the collage.	0 1 2 3 4 5 6
LAYOUT	▪ Thoughtful manipulation of text, graphics, and layout reflects and develops the purpose. Text, if used, is strategically placed to enhance meaning. Successful use of overlapping and emphasis encourages greater understanding of message.	0 1 2 3 4 5 6
MATERIALS	▪ Unique and original use of a variety of materials is consistent to the purpose of the collage.	0 1 2 3 4 5 6
ELEMENTS AND PRINCIPLES OF DESIGN	▪ Elements of design (i.e., line, shape, size, texture, and color) and principles of design (i.e., balance, repetition, contrast, harmony, emphasis, and unity) are successfully and effectively presented to communicate the message/topic.	0 1 2 3 4 5 6
CREATIVITY	▪ Individual insight is originally expressed in relation to the content.	0 1 2 3 4 5 6
	▪ Individual spark is originally expressed in relation to the presentation.	0 1 2 3 4 5 6
REFLECTION	▪ Insightful reflection on the learning of the content through product development is expressed.	0 1 2 3 4 5 6
	▪ Insightful reflection on what the student learned about self as a learner is expressed.	0 1 2 3 4 5 6

Comments

Meaning of Performance Scale:

6—PROFESSIONAL LEVEL: level expected from a professional in the content area

5—ADVANCED LEVEL: level exceeds expectations of the standard

4—PROFICIENT LEVEL: level expected for meeting the standard

3—PROGRESSING LEVEL: level demonstrates movement toward the standard

2—NOVICE LEVEL: level demonstrates initial awareness and knowledge of standard

1—NONPERFORMING LEVEL: level indicates no effort made to meet standard

0—NONPARTICIPATING LEVEL: level indicates nothing turned in

GRAPH Tier 1—DAP TOOL

CONTENT	▪ Is the content correct and complete?	0 1 2 3 4 5 6
	▪ Has the content been thought about in a way that goes beyond a surface understanding?	0 1 2 3 4 5 6
	▪ Is the content put together in such a way that people understand it?	0 1 2 3 4 5 6
PRESENTATION		
TYPE/TITLE	▪ Is the type of graph appropriate for the data? Does the title describe what is shown in the graph?	0 1 2 3 4 5 6
LABELS	▪ Is each axis clearly labeled? Does each label describe the number and the unit? Are the labels in a good place?	0 1 2 3 4 5 6
DATA	▪ Is the scale for each axis appropriate? Are the numbers and units accurate? Do they clearly show the intent of the graph?	0 1 2 3 4 5 6
INTERPRETATION	▪ Have the data been interpreted correctly? Do the observations correspond to the data?	0 1 2 3 4 5 6
VARIABLES (OPTIONAL)	▪ Are the independent and dependent variables identified clearly and correctly?	0 1 2 3 4 5 6
CREATIVITY	▪ Is the content seen in a new way?	0 1 2 3 4 5 6
	▪ Is the presentation done in a new way?	0 1 2 3 4 5 6
REFLECTION	▪ What did you learn about the content as you completed this product?	0 1 2 3 4 5 6
	▪ What did you learn about yourself as a learner by creating this product?	0 1 2 3 4 5 6

Comments

_____

_____

Meaning of Performance Scale:

6—PROFESSIONAL LEVEL: level expected from a professional in the content area

5—ADVANCED LEVEL: level exceeds expectations of the standard

4—PROFICIENT LEVEL: level expected for meeting the standard

3—PROGRESSING LEVEL: level demonstrates movement toward the standard

2—NOVICE LEVEL: level demonstrates initial awareness and knowledge of standard

1—NONPERFORMING LEVEL: level indicates no effort made to meet standard

0—NONPARTICIPATING LEVEL: level indicates nothing turned in

Visual Products

GRAPH Tier 2—DAP TOOL

CONTENT	▪ Content is accurate.	0 1 2 3 4 5 6
	▪ Content has depth and complexity of thought.	0 1 2 3 4 5 6
	▪ Content is organized.	0 1 2 3 4 5 6
PRESENTATION		
TYPE/TITLE	▪ The type of graph is best suited for the data. Title is clearly indicative of the data displayed.	0 1 2 3 4 5 6
LABELS	▪ Each axis is specifically and concisely labeled. Each label clearly describes both the number and the unit. Placement of the labels aids understanding.	0 1 2 3 4 5 6
DATA	▪ The scale for each axis is best suited for the data. Both the numbers and units are accurately calculated and displayed. They fully show the intended relationship.	0 1 2 3 4 5 6
INTERPRETATION	▪ The data have been interpreted fully. The observations clearly correspond.	0 1 2 3 4 5 6
VARIABLES (OPTIONAL)	▪ The independent and dependent variables are accurately and appropriately identified to aid in understanding the data.	0 1 2 3 4 5 6
CREATIVITY	▪ Individual insight is expressed in relation to the content.	0 1 2 3 4 5 6
	▪ Individual spark is expressed in relation to the presentation.	0 1 2 3 4 5 6
REFLECTION	▪ Reflection on the learning of the content through product development is apparent.	0 1 2 3 4 5 6
	▪ Reflection on what the student learned about self as a learner is apparent.	0 1 2 3 4 5 6

Comments

_____

_____

Meaning of Performance Scale:

6—PROFESSIONAL LEVEL: level expected from a professional in the content area

5—ADVANCED LEVEL: level exceeds expectations of the standard

4—PROFICIENT LEVEL: level expected for meeting the standard

3—PROGRESSING LEVEL: level demonstrates movement toward the standard

2—NOVICE LEVEL: level demonstrates initial awareness and knowledge of standard

1—NONPERFORMING LEVEL: level indicates no effort made to meet standard

0—NONPARTICIPATING LEVEL: level indicates nothing turned in

GRAPH Tier 3—DAP TOOL

CONTENT	▪ Content is accurate and thorough in detail.	0 1 2 3 4 5 6
	▪ Product shows complex understanding and manipulation of content.	0 1 2 3 4 5 6
	▪ Product shows deep probing of content.	0 1 2 3 4 5 6
	▪ Organization is best suited to the product.	0 1 2 3 4 5 6
PRESENTATION		
TYPE/TITLE	▪ The type of graph enhances the display and interpretation of the data. Title enhances the purpose of the data displayed.	0 1 2 3 4 5 6
LABELS	▪ Labels accurately and effectively describe each axis, number, and unit. Placement of the labels enhances understanding.	0 1 2 3 4 5 6
DATA	▪ The scale for each axis naturally represents the data and also enhances the interpretation of the data. Numbers and percentages are not only accurately calculated, but they also are effectively positioned. They clearly show relationships.	0 1 2 3 4 5 6
INTERPRETATION	▪ The data have been insightfully interpreted, clearly linking data to observations.	0 1 2 3 4 5 6
VARIABLES (OPTIONAL)	▪ Both the independent and dependent variables fully describe the intent of the data so that interpretation is clear.	0 1 2 3 4 5 6
CREATIVITY	▪ Individual insight is originally expressed in relation to the content.	0 1 2 3 4 5 6
	▪ Individual spark is originally expressed in relation to the presentation.	0 1 2 3 4 5 6
REFLECTION	▪ Insightful reflection on the learning of the content through product development is expressed.	0 1 2 3 4 5 6
	▪ Insightful reflection on what the student learned about self as a learner is expressed.	0 1 2 3 4 5 6

Comments

_____

_____

Meaning of Performance Scale:

6—PROFESSIONAL LEVEL: level expected from a professional in the content area

5—ADVANCED LEVEL: level exceeds expectations of the standard

4—PROFICIENT LEVEL: level expected for meeting the standard

3—PROGRESSING LEVEL: level demonstrates movement toward the standard

2—NOVICE LEVEL: level demonstrates initial awareness and knowledge of standard

1—NONPERFORMING LEVEL: level indicates no effort made to meet standard

0—NONPARTICIPATING LEVEL: level indicates nothing turned in

Visual Products

PAMPHLET Tier 1—DAP TOOL

CONTENT		
	▪ Is the content correct and complete?	0 1 2 3 4 5 6
	▪ Has the content been thought about in a way that goes beyond a surface understanding?	0 1 2 3 4 5 6
	▪ Is the content put together in such a way that people understand it?	0 1 2 3 4 5 6
PRESENTATION		
TEXT	▪ Is the title clear? Does the text explain the topic?	0 1 2 3 4 5 6
GRAPHICS	▪ Are the graphics (illustrations, photos) important to the topic? Are the graphics and text balanced?	0 1 2 3 4 5 6
LAYOUT	▪ Do the pamphlet folds increase reader understanding? Is the pamphlet pleasing to the eye?	0 1 2 3 4 5 6
CREATIVITY	▪ Is the content seen in a new way?	0 1 2 3 4 5 6
	▪ Is the presentation done in a new way?	0 1 2 3 4 5 6
REFLECTION	▪ What did you learn about the content as you completed this product?	0 1 2 3 4 5 6
	▪ What did you learn about yourself as a learner by creating this product?	0 1 2 3 4 5 6

Comments

_____

_____

Meaning of Performance Scale:

6—PROFESSIONAL LEVEL: level expected from a professional in the content area

5—ADVANCED LEVEL: level exceeds expectations of the standard

4—PROFICIENT LEVEL: level expected for meeting the standard

3—PROGRESSING LEVEL: level demonstrates movement toward the standard

2—NOVICE LEVEL: level demonstrates initial awareness and knowledge of standard

1—NONPERFORMING LEVEL: level indicates no effort made to meet standard

0—NONPARTICIPATING LEVEL: level indicates nothing turned in

Note. Adapted from *Strategies for Differentiating Instruction: Best Practices for the Classroom* (p. 143), by J. L. Roberts and T. F. Inman, 2007, Waco, TX: Prufrock Press. Copyright © 2007 by Prufrock Press. Adapted with permission.

PAMPHLET Tier 2—DAP TOOL

CONTENT		
	▪ Content is accurate.	0 1 2 3 4 5 6
	▪ Content has depth and complexity of thought.	0 1 2 3 4 5 6
	▪ Content is organized.	0 1 2 3 4 5 6
PRESENTATION		
TEXT	▪ Title enhances the pamphlet. Text highlights most important concepts in topic.	0 1 2 3 4 5 6
GRAPHICS	▪ Graphics (illustrations, photos) add information to the topic.	0 1 2 3 4 5 6
LAYOUT	▪ Layout design is organized and attractive. Multifold design showcases graphics and text. It is pleasing to the eye.	0 1 2 3 4 5 6
CREATIVITY	▪ Individual insight is expressed in relation to the content.	0 1 2 3 4 5 6
	▪ Individual spark is expressed in relation to the presentation.	0 1 2 3 4 5 6
REFLECTION	▪ Reflection on the learning of the content through product development is apparent.	0 1 2 3 4 5 6
	▪ Reflection on what the student learned about self as a learner is apparent.	0 1 2 3 4 5 6

Comments

_____

_____

Meaning of Performance Scale:

6—PROFESSIONAL LEVEL: level expected from a professional in the content area

5—ADVANCED LEVEL: level exceeds expectations of the standard

4—PROFICIENT LEVEL: level expected for meeting the standard

3—PROGRESSING LEVEL: level demonstrates movement toward the standard

2—NOVICE LEVEL: level demonstrates initial awareness and knowledge of standard

1—NONPERFORMING LEVEL: level indicates no effort made to meet standard

0—NONPARTICIPATING LEVEL: level indicates nothing turned in

Note. Adapted from *Strategies for Differentiating Instruction: Best Practices for the Classroom* (p. 144), by J. L. Roberts and T. F. Inman, 2007, Waco, TX: Prufrock Press. Copyright © 2007 by Prufrock Press. Adapted with permission.

Visual Products

PAMPHLET Tier 3—DAP TOOL

CONTENT		
	▪ Content is accurate and thorough in detail.	0 1 2 3 4 5 6
	▪ Product shows complex understanding and manipulation of content.	0 1 2 3 4 5 6
	▪ Product shows deep probing of content.	0 1 2 3 4 5 6
	▪ Organization is best suited to the product.	0 1 2 3 4 5 6
PRESENTATION		
TEXT	▪ Title reflects purpose. Text highlights most important concepts in clear, concise manner.	0 1 2 3 4 5 6
GRAPHICS	▪ Graphics (illustrations, photos) enhance meaning.	0 1 2 3 4 5 6
LAYOUT	▪ Thoughtful manipulation of color, layout, and font reflects purpose. Multifold design enhances readability and meaning. It is pleasing to the eye.	0 1 2 3 4 5 6
CREATIVITY	▪ Individual insight is originally expressed in relation to the content.	0 1 2 3 4 5 6
	▪ Individual spark is originally expressed in relation to the presentation.	0 1 2 3 4 5 6
REFLECTION	▪ Insightful reflection on the learning of the content through product development is expressed.	0 1 2 3 4 5 6
	▪ Insightful reflection on what the student learned about self as a learner is expressed.	0 1 2 3 4 5 6

Comments

_____

_____

Meaning of Performance Scale:

6—PROFESSIONAL LEVEL: level expected from a professional in the content area

5—ADVANCED LEVEL: level exceeds expectations of the standard

4—PROFICIENT LEVEL: level expected for meeting the standard

3—PROGRESSING LEVEL: level demonstrates movement toward the standard

2—NOVICE LEVEL: level demonstrates initial awareness and knowledge of standard

1—NONPERFORMING LEVEL: level indicates no effort made to meet standard

0—NONPARTICIPATING LEVEL: level indicates nothing turned in

Note. Adapted from _Strategies for Differentiating Instruction: Best Practices for the Classroom_ (p. 145), by J. L. Roberts and T. F. Inman, 2007, Waco, TX: Prufrock Press. Copyright © 2007 by Prufrock Press. Adapted with permission.

Visual Products

PIE CHART Tier 1—DAP TOOL

CONTENT	▪ Is the content correct and complete?	0 1 2 3 4 5 6
	▪ Has the content been thought about in a way that goes beyond a surface understanding?	0 1 2 3 4 5 6
	▪ Is the content put together in such a way that people understand it?	0 1 2 3 4 5 6
PRESENTATION		
TYPE/TITLE	▪ Does the title describe what is shown in the graph? Is the pie graph the best way to present this information?	0 1 2 3 4 5 6
LABELS	▪ Is every section of the circle clearly labeled? Does each label describe the number and the unit? Are the labels in a good place?	0 1 2 3 4 5 6
DATA RANGE	▪ Are the numbers and percentages accurate? Do they clearly show the parts-to-whole relationship?	0 1 2 3 4 5 6
DESIGN	▪ Is the circle well drawn? Is there an appropriate number of sections without being too many or unclear? Are the sections of the circle drawn to represent percentages? Is color or pattern used to show that one section differs from another?	0 1 2 3 4 5 6
CREATIVITY	▪ Is the content seen in a new way?	0 1 2 3 4 5 6
	▪ Is the presentation done in a new way?	0 1 2 3 4 5 6
REFLECTION	▪ What did you learn about the content as you completed this product?	0 1 2 3 4 5 6
	▪ What did you learn about yourself as a learner by creating this product?	0 1 2 3 4 5 6

Comments

_____

_____

Meaning of Performance Scale:

6—PROFESSIONAL LEVEL: level expected from a professional in the content area

5—ADVANCED LEVEL: level exceeds expectations of the standard

4—PROFICIENT LEVEL: level expected for meeting the standard

3—PROGRESSING LEVEL: level demonstrates movement toward the standard

2—NOVICE LEVEL: level demonstrates initial awareness and knowledge of standard

1—NONPERFORMING LEVEL: level indicates no effort made to meet standard

0—NONPARTICIPATING LEVEL: level indicates nothing turned in

Visual Products

PIE CHART Tier 2—DAP TOOL

CONTENT	▪ Content is accurate.	0 1 2 3 4 5 6
	▪ Content has depth and complexity of thought.	0 1 2 3 4 5 6
	▪ Content is organized.	0 1 2 3 4 5 6
PRESENTATION		
TYPE/TITLE	▪ Title is clearly indicative of the data displayed. The pie graph is best suited for the data.	0 1 2 3 4 5 6
LABELS	▪ Each circle section is clearly and concisely labeled. Each label clearly describes both the number and the unit. Placement of the labels aids in understanding.	0 1 2 3 4 5 6
DATA RANGE	▪ Both the numbers and percentages are accurately calculated and displayed. They fully show the parts-to-whole relationship.	0 1 2 3 4 5 6
DESIGN	▪ The circle and the sections are accurately and proportionally drawn. Sections clearly indicate the correct percentages and relationships. Colors or patterns are used to effectively differentiate sections.	0 1 2 3 4 5 6
CREATIVITY	▪ Individual insight is expressed in relation to the content.	0 1 2 3 4 5 6
	▪ Individual spark is expressed in relation to the presentation.	0 1 2 3 4 5 6
REFLECTION	▪ Reflection on the learning of the content through product development is apparent.	0 1 2 3 4 5 6
	▪ Reflection on what the student learned about self as a learner is apparent.	0 1 2 3 4 5 6

Comments

Meaning of Performance Scale:

6—PROFESSIONAL LEVEL: level expected from a professional in the content area

5—ADVANCED LEVEL: level exceeds expectations of the standard

4—PROFICIENT LEVEL: level expected for meeting the standard

3—PROGRESSING LEVEL: level demonstrates movement toward the standard

2—NOVICE LEVEL: level demonstrates initial awareness and knowledge of standard

1—NONPERFORMING LEVEL: level indicates no effort made to meet standard

0—NONPARTICIPATING LEVEL: level indicates nothing turned in

PIE CHART Tier 3—DAP TOOL

CONTENT		
	▪ Content is accurate and thorough in detail.	0 1 2 3 4 5 6
	▪ Product shows complex understanding and manipulation of content.	0 1 2 3 4 5 6
	▪ Product shows deep probing of content.	0 1 2 3 4 5 6
	▪ Organization is best suited to the product.	0 1 2 3 4 5 6
PRESENTATION		
TYPE/TITLE	▪ Title enhances the purpose of the data displayed. The pie graph is ideally suited for the data.	0 1 2 3 4 5 6
LABELS	▪ Labels accurately and effectively describe each section, number, and unit. Placement of the labels enhances understanding.	0 1 2 3 4 5 6
DATA RANGE	▪ Numbers and percentages are not only accurately calculated, but they also are effectively positioned. They inarguably show the parts-to-whole relationship.	0 1 2 3 4 5 6
DESIGN	▪ The circle and the sections are accurately and proportionally drawn so that interpretation of the data is ensured. Sections completely indicate the correct percentages and relationships. Colors or patterns enhance the meaning.	0 1 2 3 4 5 6
CREATIVITY	▪ Individual insight is originally expressed in relation to the content.	0 1 2 3 4 5 6
	▪ Individual spark is originally expressed in relation to the presentation.	0 1 2 3 4 5 6
REFLECTION	▪ Insightful reflection on the learning of the content through product development is expressed.	0 1 2 3 4 5 6
	▪ Insightful reflection on what the student learned about self as a learner is expressed.	0 1 2 3 4 5 6

Comments

_____

_____

Meaning of Performance Scale:

6—PROFESSIONAL LEVEL: level expected from a professional in the content area

5—ADVANCED LEVEL: level exceeds expectations of the standard

4—PROFICIENT LEVEL: level expected for meeting the standard

3—PROGRESSING LEVEL: level demonstrates movement toward the standard

2—NOVICE LEVEL: level demonstrates initial awareness and knowledge of standard

1—NONPERFORMING LEVEL: level indicates no effort made to meet standard

0—NONPARTICIPATING LEVEL: level indicates nothing turned in

POLITICAL CARTOON Tier 1—DAP TOOL

CONTENT	▪ Is the content correct and complete?	0 1 2 3 4 5 6
	▪ Has the content been thought about in a way that goes beyond a surface understanding?	0 1 2 3 4 5 6
	▪ Is the content put together in such a way that people understand it?	0 1 2 3 4 5 6
PRESENTATION		
PURPOSE	▪ Does the cartoon make a statement about something in the world, past or present? Does it include humor or sarcasm? Will the audience understand the reference? Is it respectful of people's rights?	0 1 2 3 4 5 6
ILLUSTRATION	▪ Is the illustration clear and easy to understand? Does the illustration help the reader understand the message? Does it include symbolism or a caricature? Could the illustration stand alone without text?	0 1 2 3 4 5 6
LAYOUT	▪ Is the cartoon a single cell or does it have multiple cells? Is it the best number to get across the purpose?	0 1 2 3 4 5 6
TEXT (OPTIONAL)	▪ Is the title clear? If used, are the character balloons easy to read? Is the text to the point and clear? Does it make a statement about something that is happening or has happened in the world?	0 1 2 3 4 5 6
CREATIVITY	▪ Is the content seen in a new way?	0 1 2 3 4 5 6
	▪ Is the presentation done in a new way?	0 1 2 3 4 5 6
REFLECTION	▪ What did you learn about the content as you completed this product?	0 1 2 3 4 5 6
	▪ What did you learn about yourself as a learner by creating this product?	0 1 2 3 4 5 6

Comments

_____

_____

Meaning of Performance Scale:
6—PROFESSIONAL LEVEL: level expected from a professional in the content area
5—ADVANCED LEVEL: level exceeds expectations of the standard
4—PROFICIENT LEVEL: level expected for meeting the standard
3—PROGRESSING LEVEL: level demonstrates movement toward the standard
2—NOVICE LEVEL: level demonstrates initial awareness and knowledge of standard
1—NONPERFORMING LEVEL: level indicates no effort made to meet standard
0—NONPARTICIPATING LEVEL: level indicates nothing turned in

POLITICAL CARTOON Tier 2—DAP TOOL

CONTENT	• Content is accurate.	0 1 2 3 4 5 6
	• Content has depth and complexity of thought.	0 1 2 3 4 5 6
	• Content is organized.	0 1 2 3 4 5 6
PRESENTATION		
PURPOSE	• The cartoon is designed for a specific audience as evidenced in text, illustration, and layout. The intended audience will understand the cartoonist's view about a contemporary or historical event, person, or situation. It fully respects others' rights.	0 1 2 3 4 5 6
ILLUSTRATION	• The illustration enhances or embodies the purpose. It aids the reader's understanding through use of symbolism, caricature, or carefully chosen images. The illustration alone could depict the purpose.	0 1 2 3 4 5 6
LAYOUT	• Whether single- or multicelled, the layout enhances the understanding of the cartoon.	0 1 2 3 4 5 6
TEXT (OPTIONAL)	• Title enhances the cartoon. The text clearly and concisely establishes the cartoonist's viewpoint. The text is relevant to the purpose. If used, character balloons are effectively incorporated.	0 1 2 3 4 5 6
CREATIVITY	• Individual insight is expressed in relation to the content.	0 1 2 3 4 5 6
	• Individual spark is expressed in relation to the presentation.	0 1 2 3 4 5 6
REFLECTION	• Reflection on the learning of the content through product development is apparent.	0 1 2 3 4 5 6
	• Reflection on what the student learned about self as a learner is apparent.	0 1 2 3 4 5 6

Comments

_____

_____

Meaning of Performance Scale:

6—PROFESSIONAL LEVEL: level expected from a professional in the content area

5—ADVANCED LEVEL: level exceeds expectations of the standard

4—PROFICIENT LEVEL: level expected for meeting the standard

3—PROGRESSING LEVEL: level demonstrates movement toward the standard

2—NOVICE LEVEL: level demonstrates initial awareness and knowledge of standard

1—NONPERFORMING LEVEL: level indicates no effort made to meet standard

0—NONPARTICIPATING LEVEL: level indicates nothing turned in

Visual Products

POLITICAL CARTOON Tier 3—DAP TOOL

CONTENT	▪ Content is accurate and thorough in detail.	0 1 2 3 4 5 6
	▪ Product shows complex understanding and manipulation of content.	0 1 2 3 4 5 6
	▪ Product shows deep probing of content.	0 1 2 3 4 5 6
	▪ Organization is best suited to the product.	0 1 2 3 4 5 6
PRESENTATION		
PURPOSE	▪ The cartoon is carefully created for a specific contemporary audience. The text, illustration, and layout all fully support the specific viewpoint of the cartoonist in regard to a current or historical event, person, or situation. Others' rights are respected and honored.	0 1 2 3 4 5 6
ILLUSTRATION	▪ The cartoonist's viewpoint is inherent in the illustration. It plays an integral role in the reader's understanding of the current or historical event, person, or situation through its skillful use of symbolism, caricature, or well-chosen images. Without the illustration, the cartoon loses much of its meaning.	0 1 2 3 4 5 6
LAYOUT	▪ The number and arrangement of cells purposely support and further the cartoon's meaning.	0 1 2 3 4 5 6
TEXT *(OPTIONAL)*	▪ Title and text enhance the purpose of the cartoon in a concise yet clear manner. If used, character balloons enhance the overall meaning of the cartoon.	0 1 2 3 4 5 6
CREATIVITY	▪ Individual insight is originally expressed in relation to the content.	0 1 2 3 4 5 6
	▪ Individual spark is originally expressed in relation to the presentation.	0 1 2 3 4 5 6
REFLECTION	▪ Insightful reflection on the learning of the content through product development is expressed.	0 1 2 3 4 5 6
	▪ Insightful reflection on what the student learned about self as a learner is expressed.	0 1 2 3 4 5 6

Comments

Meaning of Performance Scale:

6—PROFESSIONAL LEVEL: level expected from a professional in the content area

5—ADVANCED LEVEL: level exceeds expectations of the standard

4—PROFICIENT LEVEL: level expected for meeting the standard

3—PROGRESSING LEVEL: level demonstrates movement toward the standard

2—NOVICE LEVEL: level demonstrates initial awareness and knowledge of standard

1—NONPERFORMING LEVEL: level indicates no effort made to meet standard

0—NONPARTICIPATING LEVEL: level indicates nothing turned in

Visual Products

POSTER Tier 1—DAP TOOL

CONTENT	▪ Is the content correct and complete?	0 1 2 3 4 5 6
	▪ Has the content been thought about in a way that goes beyond a surface understanding?	0 1 2 3 4 5 6
	▪ Is the content put together in such a way that people understand it?	0 1 2 3 4 5 6
PRESENTATION		
TEXT	▪ Is the title easy to see, clear, and well placed? Do the labels clearly explain the graphics?	0 1 2 3 4 5 6
GRAPHICS	▪ Are the graphics (illustrations, photos) important and relevant to the topic?	0 1 2 3 4 5 6
LAYOUT	▪ Are the images carefully selected and emphasized? Is the labeling linked to the graphic? Is it pleasing to the eye? Is the spacing deliberate to draw attention to main parts of the poster?	0 1 2 3 4 5 6
CREATIVITY	▪ Is the content seen in a new way?	0 1 2 3 4 5 6
	▪ Is the presentation done in a new way?	0 1 2 3 4 5 6
REFLECTION	▪ What did you learn about the content as you completed this product?	0 1 2 3 4 5 6
	▪ What did you learn about yourself as a learner by creating this product?	0 1 2 3 4 5 6

Comments

_____

_____

Meaning of Performance Scale:

6—PROFESSIONAL LEVEL: level expected from a professional in the content area

5—ADVANCED LEVEL: level exceeds expectations of the standard

4—PROFICIENT LEVEL: level expected for meeting the standard

3—PROGRESSING LEVEL: level demonstrates movement toward the standard

2—NOVICE LEVEL: level demonstrates initial awareness and knowledge of standard

1—NONPERFORMING LEVEL: level indicates no effort made to meet standard

0—NONPARTICIPATING LEVEL: level indicates nothing turned in

Visual Products

POSTER Tier 2—DAP TOOL

CONTENT	▪ Content is accurate.	0 1 2 3 4 5 6
	▪ Content has depth and complexity of thought.	0 1 2 3 4 5 6
	▪ Content is organized.	0 1 2 3 4 5 6
PRESENTATION		
TEXT	▪ Title enhances the poster's purpose and is well placed. Text highlights most important concepts in topic.	0 1 2 3 4 5 6
GRAPHICS	▪ Graphics (illustrations, photos) add information and are appropriate for the topic.	0 1 2 3 4 5 6
LAYOUT	▪ Layout design clearly emphasizes graphics in an organized and attractive manner. Text is placed to clearly describe/explain all graphic images. Spacing is carefully planned with consideration of space not used.	0 1 2 3 4 5 6
CREATIVITY	▪ Individual insight is expressed in relation to the content.	0 1 2 3 4 5 6
	▪ Individual spark is expressed in relation to the presentation.	0 1 2 3 4 5 6
REFLECTION	▪ Reflection on the learning of the content through product development is apparent.	0 1 2 3 4 5 6
	▪ Reflection on what the student learned about self as a learner is apparent.	0 1 2 3 4 5 6

Comments

Meaning of Performance Scale:

6—PROFESSIONAL LEVEL: level expected from a professional in the content area

5—ADVANCED LEVEL: level exceeds expectations of the standard

4—PROFICIENT LEVEL: level expected for meeting the standard

3—PROGRESSING LEVEL: level demonstrates movement toward the standard

2—NOVICE LEVEL: level demonstrates initial awareness and knowledge of standard

1—NONPERFORMING LEVEL: level indicates no effort made to meet standard

0—NONPARTICIPATING LEVEL: level indicates nothing turned in

POSTER Tier 3—DAP TOOL

CONTENT		• Content is accurate and thorough in detail.	0 1 2 3 4 5 6
		• Product shows complex understanding and manipulation of content.	0 1 2 3 4 5 6
		• Product shows deep probing of content.	0 1 2 3 4 5 6
		• Organization is best suited to the product.	0 1 2 3 4 5 6
PRESENTATION			
	TEXT	• Title, clearly reflecting purpose, is strategically placed. Text highlights most important concepts in clear, concise manner.	0 1 2 3 4 5 6
	GRAPHICS	• Graphics (illustrations, photos) enhance meaning and are best suited for the purpose.	0 1 2 3 4 5 6
	LAYOUT	• Successful composition of graphic images and design concepts communicates the purpose. Text is strategically placed to enhance the message of the poster. Negative space is used to highlight key points.	0 1 2 3 4 5 6
CREATIVITY		• Individual insight is originally expressed in relation to the content.	0 1 2 3 4 5 6
		• Individual spark is originally expressed in relation to the presentation.	0 1 2 3 4 5 6
REFLECTION		• Insightful reflection on the learning of the content through product development is expressed.	0 1 2 3 4 5 6
		• Insightful reflection on what the student learned about self as a learner is expressed.	0 1 2 3 4 5 6

Visual Products

Comments

_____

_____

Meaning of Performance Scale:

6—PROFESSIONAL LEVEL: level expected from a professional in the content area

5—ADVANCED LEVEL: level exceeds expectations of the standard

4—PROFICIENT LEVEL: level expected for meeting the standard

3—PROGRESSING LEVEL: level demonstrates movement toward the standard

2—NOVICE LEVEL: level demonstrates initial awareness and knowledge of standard

1—NONPERFORMING LEVEL: level indicates no effort made to meet standard

0—NONPARTICIPATING LEVEL: level indicates nothing turned in

DBQ (Document-Based Question) Tier 1—DAP TOOL

CONTENT	▪ Is the content correct and complete?	0 1 2 3 4 5 6
	▪ Has the content been thought about in a way that goes beyond a surface understanding?	0 1 2 3 4 5 6
	▪ Is the content put together in such a way that people understand it?	0 1 2 3 4 5 6
PRESENTATION		
STRUCTURE AND THESIS	▪ Is there a strong introduction? Have time and place been established? Does the DBQ contain a well-worded thesis that is developed and supported? Does the thesis address the task? Is the essay logically organized into well-developed paragraphs? Do transitions lead from one section to another? Does each paragraph have one main idea? Does the essay come to a close and link back to the thesis?	0 1 2 3 4 5 6
ARGUMENT	▪ Has important outside knowledge been applied to the information provided? Does the argument include comparison and historical analysis? Is the argument soundly based on the documents? Have all parts of the task been addressed logically?	0 1 2 3 4 5 6
SUPPORTING EVIDENCE	▪ Have primary and secondary sources been evaluated and interpreted correctly? Have historical sources been incorporated carefully and appropriately? Is that information important and reliable? Is the evidence analyzed and not just listed? Does all information relate to the thesis? Has the thesis been proven through supporting details and explanation? Have the texts been used carefully and appropriately? Have multiple perspectives been addressed?	0 1 2 3 4 5 6
CORRECTNESS	▪ Is the DBQ free from usage, punctuation, capitalization, and spelling errors? Are sources cited correctly?	0 1 2 3 4 5 6
CREATIVITY	▪ Is the content seen in a new way?	0 1 2 3 4 5 6
	▪ Is the presentation done in a new way?	0 1 2 3 4 5 6
REFLECTION	▪ What did you learn about the content as you completed this product?	0 1 2 3 4 5 6
	▪ What did you learn about yourself as a learner by creating this product?	0 1 2 3 4 5 6

Comments

_____

_____

Meaning of Performance Scale:

6—PROFESSIONAL LEVEL: level expected from a professional in the content area

5—ADVANCED LEVEL: level exceeds expectations of the standard

4—PROFICIENT LEVEL: level expected for meeting the standard

3—PROGRESSING LEVEL: level demonstrates movement toward the standard

2—NOVICE LEVEL: level demonstrates initial awareness and knowledge of standard

1—NONPERFORMING LEVEL: level indicates no effort made to meet standard

0—NONPARTICIPATING LEVEL: level indicates nothing turned in

DBQ (Document-Based Question) Tier 2—DAP TOOL

CONTENT	• Content is accurate.	0 1 2 3 4 5 6
	• Content has depth and complexity of thought.	0 1 2 3 4 5 6
	• Content is organized.	0 1 2 3 4 5 6
PRESENTATION		
STRUCTURE AND THESIS	• The introduction clearly gains the audience's interest. Time and place are discussed. The well-developed thesis is clear and addresses the task. Strong transitions between paragraphs and sections link to the purpose. Each paragraph is fully developed and logical in its organization. The conclusion pulls together all aspects of the writing and clearly links to the thesis.	0 1 2 3 4 5 6
ARGUMENT	• Accurate, appropriate, and pertinent information not included in the documents is incorporated into the argument. Both comparison and historical analysis are fully utilized. All arguments are based on valid interpretation of the documents coupled with previous knowledge. Each aspect of the task has been analyzed fully.	0 1 2 3 4 5 6
SUPPORTING EVIDENCE	• Reliable, valid, and pertinent information has been gleaned from both primary and secondary documents. Support is elaborate and detailed; it is analyzed, not just mentioned. Each idea is fully developed and relates back to the thesis. A strong balance of general ideas and specific details creates a fluid discussion. Evidence includes outside knowledge. Sources fully elaborate on or support the idea and are smoothly incorporated into the writing.	0 1 2 3 4 5 6
CORRECTNESS	• The DBQ is free from punctuation, usage, capitalization, and spelling errors. Outside sources are cited correctly.	0 1 2 3 4 5 6
CREATIVITY	• Individual insight is expressed in relation to the content.	0 1 2 3 4 5 6
	• Individual spark is expressed in relation to the presentation.	0 1 2 3 4 5 6
REFLECTION	• Reflection on the learning of the content through product development is apparent.	0 1 2 3 4 5 6
	• Reflection on what the student learned about self as a learner is apparent.	0 1 2 3 4 5 6

Comments

Meaning of Performance Scale:

6—PROFESSIONAL LEVEL: level expected from a professional in the content area

5—ADVANCED LEVEL: level exceeds expectations of the standard

4—PROFICIENT LEVEL: level expected for meeting the standard

3—PROGRESSING LEVEL: level demonstrates movement toward the standard

2—NOVICE LEVEL: level demonstrates initial awareness and knowledge of standard

1—NONPERFORMING LEVEL: level indicates no effort made to meet standard

0—NONPARTICIPATING LEVEL: level indicates nothing turned in

Written Products

DBQ (Document-Based Question) Tier 3—DAP TOOL

CONTENT		
	▪ Content is accurate and thorough in detail.	0 1 2 3 4 5 6
	▪ Product shows complex understanding and manipulation of content.	0 1 2 3 4 5 6
	▪ Product shows deep probing of content.	0 1 2 3 4 5 6
	▪ Organization is best suited to the product.	0 1 2 3 4 5 6

PRESENTATION

STRUCTURE AND THESIS	▪ The introduction cleverly gains the audience's interest. Time and place have been artfully interwoven. The thesis of the writing is original and creative, clearly guiding the entire DBQ. Sophisticated transitions between paragraphs and sections subtly link all aspects together. Sections fully develop key concepts or ideas critical to the thesis. Conclusion refers back to the thesis and summarizes pertinent information. The significance of the conclusion is clear.	0 1 2 3 4 5 6
ARGUMENT	▪ The most pertinent information not included in the documents is cleverly and accurately incorporated into the argument. Comparison, explication, and historical analysis develop the argument. All arguments stem from valid, insightful interpretation of the documents coupled with pertinent prior knowledge. Each aspect of the task has been analyzed completely.	0 1 2 3 4 5 6
SUPPORTING EVIDENCE	▪ Reliable, valid, and pertinent information has been carefully explicated from both the primary and secondary documents. Well-detailed support and elaboration are incorporated into analysis and argument. Each idea is thoroughly substantiated through pertinent detail or analyzed support. Strong, elaborate support proves thesis. Text is carefully selected and fully elaborates on or supports the thesis; its inclusion is seamless. DBQ anticipates the audience's possible misunderstandings and handles complex ideas clearly.	0 1 2 3 4 5 6
CORRECTNESS	▪ In spite of the complexity of the syntax, diction, and punctuation, the essay is free from errors. Sources are cited correctly.	0 1 2 3 4 5 6

CREATIVITY		
	▪ Individual insight is originally expressed in relation to the content.	0 1 2 3 4 5 6
	▪ Individual spark is originally expressed in relation to the presentation.	0 1 2 3 4 5 6

REFLECTION		
	▪ Insightful reflection on the learning of the content through product development is expressed.	0 1 2 3 4 5 6
	▪ Insightful reflection on what the student learned about self as a learner is expressed.	0 1 2 3 4 5 6

Comments

_____

_____

Meaning of Performance Scale:

6—PROFESSIONAL LEVEL: level expected from a professional in the content area

5—ADVANCED LEVEL: level exceeds expectations of the standard

4—PROFICIENT LEVEL: level expected for meeting the standard

3—PROGRESSING LEVEL: level demonstrates movement toward the standard

2—NOVICE LEVEL: level demonstrates initial awareness and knowledge of standard

1—NONPERFORMING LEVEL: level indicates no effort made to meet standard

0—NONPARTICIPATING LEVEL: level indicates nothing turned in

DIARY Tier 1—DAP TOOL

CONTENT	▪ Is the content correct and complete?	0 1 2 3 4 5 6
	▪ Has the content been thought about in a way that goes beyond a surface understanding?	0 1 2 3 4 5 6
	▪ Is the content put together in such a way that people understand it?	0 1 2 3 4 5 6
PRESENTATION		
TEXT	▪ Is the purpose clear? Are the entries appropriate for the assignment? Are the entries appropriate for the person/character writing them? Do the entries contain emotions and thoughts?	0 1 2 3 4 5 6
FORMAT	▪ Is it written like a diary with dates and a greeting? Does it have the right number of entries? If it is an entire diary, does it have a cover?	0 1 2 3 4 5 6
STYLE	▪ Is it written like the diarist would really write it in that the words chosen, the form of the sentences, and the expressions sound as if they came from the diarist?	0 1 2 3 4 5 6
CREATIVITY	▪ Is the content seen in a new way?	0 1 2 3 4 5 6
	▪ Is the presentation done in a new way?	0 1 2 3 4 5 6
REFLECTION	▪ What did you learn about the content as you completed this product?	0 1 2 3 4 5 6
	▪ What did you learn about yourself as a learner by creating this product?	0 1 2 3 4 5 6

Comments

_____

_____

Meaning of Performance Scale:

6—PROFESSIONAL LEVEL: level expected from a professional in the content area

5—ADVANCED LEVEL: level exceeds expectations of the standard

4—PROFICIENT LEVEL: level expected for meeting the standard

3—PROGRESSING LEVEL: level demonstrates movement toward the standard

2—NOVICE LEVEL: level demonstrates initial awareness and knowledge of standard

1—NONPERFORMING LEVEL: level indicates no effort made to meet standard

0—NONPARTICIPATING LEVEL: level indicates nothing turned in

Written Products

DIARY Tier 2—DAP TOOL

CONTENT	• Content is accurate.	0 1 2 3 4 5 6
	• Content has depth and complexity of thought.	0 1 2 3 4 5 6
	• Content is organized.	0 1 2 3 4 5 6
PRESENTATION		
TEXT	• The entries are appropriate for the assignment as to quantity and quality. The entries are emotional, thoughtful, and personal. They are authentic to the diarist as to personal reaction and reflection on the topic.	0 1 2 3 4 5 6
FORMAT	• The diary looks like a diary in that dating and greeting/closing format are used. If it is an entire diary, it has a cover consistent with the content and intent of the diary.	0 1 2 3 4 5 6
STYLE	• The diction, syntax, usage, conventions, and voice are authentic to the diarist.	0 1 2 3 4 5 6
CREATIVITY	• Individual insight is expressed in relation to the content.	0 1 2 3 4 5 6
	• Individual spark is expressed in relation to the presentation.	0 1 2 3 4 5 6
REFLECTION	• Reflection on the learning of the content through product development is apparent.	0 1 2 3 4 5 6
	• Reflection on what the student learned about self as a learner is apparent.	0 1 2 3 4 5 6

Comments

_____

_____

Meaning of Performance Scale:

6—PROFESSIONAL LEVEL: level expected from a professional in the content area

5—ADVANCED LEVEL: level exceeds expectations of the standard

4—PROFICIENT LEVEL: level expected for meeting the standard

3—PROGRESSING LEVEL: level demonstrates movement toward the standard

2—NOVICE LEVEL: level demonstrates initial awareness and knowledge of standard

1—NONPERFORMING LEVEL: level indicates no effort made to meet standard

0—NONPARTICIPATING LEVEL: level indicates nothing turned in

DIARY Tier 3—DAP TOOL

CONTENT	▪ Content is accurate and thorough in detail.	0 1 2 3 4 5 6
	▪ Product shows complex understanding and manipulation of content.	0 1 2 3 4 5 6
	▪ Product shows deep probing of content.	0 1 2 3 4 5 6
	▪ Organization is best suited to the product.	0 1 2 3 4 5 6
PRESENTATION		
TEXT	▪ The quantity and quality of the entries are best suited to the purpose. They are confessional, thoughtful, reflective, emotional, and/or analytical in nature. The content is consistent with the persona as to thought and emotion expressed.	0 1 2 3 4 5 6
FORMAT	▪ The format of the diary (i.e., cover, dates, greeting/ closing, and arrangement of entries) enhances the purpose.	0 1 2 3 4 5 6
STYLE	▪ Sophisticated manipulation of syntax, diction, usage, conventions, and voice further develops the *persona* and adds clarity and emphasis to the purpose. Every aspect of the style is authentic to the *persona*.	0 1 2 3 4 5 6
CREATIVITY	▪ Individual insight is originally expressed in relation to the content.	0 1 2 3 4 5 6
	▪ Individual spark is originally expressed in relation to the presentation.	0 1 2 3 4 5 6
REFLECTION	▪ Insightful reflection on the learning of the content through product development is expressed.	0 1 2 3 4 5 6
	▪ Insightful reflection on what the student learned about self as a learner is expressed.	0 1 2 3 4 5 6

Comments

_____

_____

Meaning of Performance Scale:

6—PROFESSIONAL LEVEL: level expected from a professional in the content area

5—ADVANCED LEVEL: level exceeds expectations of the standard

4—PROFICIENT LEVEL: level expected for meeting the standard

3—PROGRESSING LEVEL: level demonstrates movement toward the standard

2—NOVICE LEVEL: level demonstrates initial awareness and knowledge of standard

1—NONPERFORMING LEVEL: level indicates no effort made to meet standard

0—NONPARTICIPATING LEVEL: level indicates nothing turned in

Written Products

ESSAY Tier 1—DAP TOOL

CONTENT	• Is the content correct and complete?	0 1 2 3 4 5 6
	• Has the content been thought about in a way that goes beyond a surface understanding?	0 1 2 3 4 5 6
	• Is the content put together in such a way that people understand it?	0 1 2 3 4 5 6
PRESENTATION		
STRUCTURE	• Does the title link to the main idea? Is an effective attention-getting device used? Does it contain a well-worded thesis early in the paper? Is the essay organized into well-developed paragraphs? Is it logical in its organization? Do transitions lead from one section to another? Does each paragraph have one main idea? Does the essay come to a close and link back to the thesis?	0 1 2 3 4 5 6
ELABORATION AND SUPPORT	• Is there enough detail to support the ideas? Does all information relate to the thesis? Are ideas fully explained and supported? Is there a balance of general ideas with specific details? If quotes or other references are included, have they been used carefully and appropriately?	0 1 2 3 4 5 6
STYLE	• Is it written for the expected audience and purpose? Are appropriate words used? Are the sentences varied in structure? Is a suitable tone used? Is the author's voice clear? Is figurative language used in an effective way?	0 1 2 3 4 5 6
CORRECTNESS	• Is the essay free from usage, punctuation, capitalization, and spelling errors? If outside sources are used, are they cited correctly?	0 1 2 3 4 5 6
CREATIVITY	• Is the content seen in a new way?	0 1 2 3 4 5 6
	• Is the presentation done in a new way?	0 1 2 3 4 5 6
REFLECTION	• What did you learn about the content as you completed this product?	0 1 2 3 4 5 6
	• What did you learn about yourself as a learner by creating this product?	0 1 2 3 4 5 6

Comments

_____

_____

Meaning of Performance Scale:

6—PROFESSIONAL LEVEL: level expected from a professional in the content area

5—ADVANCED LEVEL: level exceeds expectations of the standard

4—PROFICIENT LEVEL: level expected for meeting the standard

3—PROGRESSING LEVEL: level demonstrates movement toward the standard

2—NOVICE LEVEL: level demonstrates initial awareness and knowledge of standard

1—NONPERFORMING LEVEL: level indicates no effort made to meet standard

0—NONPARTICIPATING LEVEL: level indicates nothing turned in

Written Products

ESSAY Tier 2—DAP TOOL

CONTENT	• Content is accurate.	0 1 2 3 4 5 6
	• Content has depth and complexity of thought.	0 1 2 3 4 5 6
	• Content is organized.	0 1 2 3 4 5 6
PRESENTATION		
STRUCTURE	• Title enhances the writing. The attention-getting device clearly gains the reader's interest. The thesis of the writing is clear and well developed. Strong transitions between paragraphs and sections link to the purpose. Each paragraph is fully developed and logical in its organization. The conclusion pulls together all aspects of the writing and clearly links to the thesis.	0 1 2 3 4 5 6
ELABORATION AND SUPPORT	• Each idea is fully developed and relates back to the thesis. A strong balance of general ideas and specific details creates a fluid discussion. Outside sources, if used, fully elaborate on or support the idea and are smoothly incorporated into the writing.	0 1 2 3 4 5 6
STYLE	• The purposeful use of varied syntax aids in the reader's understanding. Precise diction appeals to the audience and supports the purpose. Tone is consistent to purpose. Voice clearly stems from diction, syntax, and figurative language.	0 1 2 3 4 5 6
CORRECTNESS	• The essay is free from punctuation, usage, capitalization, and spelling errors. Outside sources, if used, are cited correctly.	0 1 2 3 4 5 6
CREATIVITY	• Individual insight is expressed in relation to the content.	0 1 2 3 4 5 6
	• Individual spark is expressed in relation to the presentation.	0 1 2 3 4 5 6
REFLECTION	• Reflection on the learning of the content through product development is apparent.	0 1 2 3 4 5 6
	• Reflection on what the student learned about self as a learner is apparent.	0 1 2 3 4 5 6

Comments

Meaning of Performance Scale:

6—PROFESSIONAL LEVEL: level expected from a professional in the content area

5—ADVANCED LEVEL: level exceeds expectations of the standard

4—PROFICIENT LEVEL: level expected for meeting the standard

3—PROGRESSING LEVEL: level demonstrates movement toward the standard

2—NOVICE LEVEL: level demonstrates initial awareness and knowledge of standard

1—NONPERFORMING LEVEL: level indicates no effort made to meet standard

0—NONPARTICIPATING LEVEL: level indicates nothing turned in

ESSAY Tier 3—DAP TOOL

CONTENT	▪ Content is accurate and thorough in detail.	0 1 2 3 4 5 6
	▪ Product shows complex understanding and manipulation of content.	0 1 2 3 4 5 6
	▪ Product shows deep probing of content.	0 1 2 3 4 5 6
	▪ Organization is best suited to the product.	0 1 2 3 4 5 6
PRESENTATION		
STRUCTURE	▪ Title reflects the purpose. The attention-getting device cleverly gains the reader's interest. The thesis is original and creative, clearly guiding the entire essay. Sophisticated transitions between paragraphs and sections subtly link all aspects together. Sections fully develop key concepts or ideas critical to the purpose. Conclusion refers back to the thesis and summarizes pertinent information. The significance of the conclusion is clear.	0 1 2 3 4 5 6
ELABORATION AND SUPPORT	▪ Each idea is thoroughly substantiated through pertinent detail or analyzed support. Strong, elaborate support proves main points. Outside sources, if used, are well selected and fully elaborate on or support the idea; their inclusion is seamless. Writing anticipates audience's possible misunderstandings and handles complex ideas clearly.	0 1 2 3 4 5 6
STYLE	▪ The purposeful use of varied syntax enhances the audience's understanding. Powerful diction appeals to the audience and fully supports the purpose. Voice clearly stems from tone, diction, syntax, and figurative language. Effective rhetorical devices emphasize the main ideas.	0 1 2 3 4 5 6
CORRECTNESS	▪ In spite of the complexity of the syntax, diction, and punctuation, the essay is free from errors. Outside sources, if used, are cited correctly.	0 1 2 3 4 5 6
CREATIVITY	▪ Individual insight is originally expressed in relation to the content.	0 1 2 3 4 5 6
	▪ Individual spark is originally expressed in relation to the presentation.	0 1 2 3 4 5 6
REFLECTION	▪ Insightful reflection on the learning of the content through product development is expressed.	0 1 2 3 4 5 6
	▪ Insightful reflection on what the student learned about self as a learner is expressed.	0 1 2 3 4 5 6

Comments

_____

_____

Meaning of Performance Scale:

6—PROFESSIONAL LEVEL: level expected from a professional in the content area

5—ADVANCED LEVEL: level exceeds expectations of the standard

4—PROFICIENT LEVEL: level expected for meeting the standard

3—PROGRESSING LEVEL: level demonstrates movement toward the standard

2—NOVICE LEVEL: level demonstrates initial awareness and knowledge of standard

1—NONPERFORMING LEVEL: level indicates no effort made to meet standard

0—NONPARTICIPATING LEVEL: level indicates nothing turned in

INTERVIEW (WRITTEN) Tier 1—DAP TOOL

CONTENT	• Is the content correct and complete?	0 1 2 3 4 5 6
	• Has the content been thought about in a way that goes beyond a surface understanding?	0 1 2 3 4 5 6
	• Is the content put together in such a way that people understand it?	0 1 2 3 4 5 6
PRESENTATION		
PURPOSE/ AUDIENCE	• Is the purpose clear? Is the person to be interviewed a good choice? Have you provided the questions to the interviewee in a timely manner?	0 1 2 3 4 5 6
QUESTIONS	• Have you prepared questions that are open ended with no right or wrong answers? Are they important questions that draw out information? Are they worded correctly? Are they limited in number?	0 1 2 3 4 5 6
FORMAT	• After the interview, have you rewritten the questions and answers into a dialogue or other appropriate format? Is there a strong introduction and conclusion? If you left out parts of the interview, are you explaining why you have done this?	0 1 2 3 4 5 6
CREATIVITY	• Is the content seen in a new way?	0 1 2 3 4 5 6
	• Is the presentation done in a new way?	0 1 2 3 4 5 6
REFLECTION	• What did you learn about the content as you completed this product?	0 1 2 3 4 5 6
	• What did you learn about yourself as a learner by creating this product?	0 1 2 3 4 5 6

Comments

_____

_____

Meaning of Performance Scale:

6—PROFESSIONAL LEVEL: level expected from a professional in the content area

5—ADVANCED LEVEL: level exceeds expectations of the standard

4—PROFICIENT LEVEL: level expected for meeting the standard

3—PROGRESSING LEVEL: level demonstrates movement toward the standard

2—NOVICE LEVEL: level demonstrates initial awareness and knowledge of standard

1—NONPERFORMING LEVEL: level indicates no effort made to meet standard

0—NONPARTICIPATING LEVEL: level indicates nothing turned in

Written Products

INTERVIEW (WRITTEN) Tier 2—DAP TOOL

CONTENT	▪ Content is accurate.	0 1 2 3 4 5 6
	▪ Content has depth and complexity of thought.	0 1 2 3 4 5 6
	▪ Content is organized.	0 1 2 3 4 5 6
PRESENTATION		
PURPOSE/ AUDIENCE	▪ The purpose of the interview is clear. The interviewee is highly knowledgeable about the subject. The questions are provided in an efficient way so that the interviewee has sufficient time to answer.	0 1 2 3 4 5 6
QUESTIONS	▪ Questions are pointed, open ended, and grammatically correct. They cover all main aspects of the topic.	0 1 2 3 4 5 6
FORMAT	▪ The written interview, in accurate dialogue form, is thorough and an exact rendering of the interview. Any deviations are explained. A strong introduction and conclusion emphasize the purpose.	0 1 2 3 4 5 6
CREATIVITY	▪ Individual insight is expressed in relation to the content.	0 1 2 3 4 5 6
	▪ Individual spark is expressed in relation to the presentation.	0 1 2 3 4 5 6
REFLECTION	▪ Reflection on the learning of the content through product development is apparent.	0 1 2 3 4 5 6
	▪ Reflection on what the student learned about self as a learner is apparent.	0 1 2 3 4 5 6

Comments

_____

_____

Meaning of Performance Scale:

6—PROFESSIONAL LEVEL: level expected from a professional in the content area

5—ADVANCED LEVEL: level exceeds expectations of the standard

4—PROFICIENT LEVEL: level expected for meeting the standard

3—PROGRESSING LEVEL: level demonstrates movement toward the standard

2—NOVICE LEVEL: level demonstrates initial awareness and knowledge of standard

1—NONPERFORMING LEVEL: level indicates no effort made to meet standard

0—NONPARTICIPATING LEVEL: level indicates nothing turned in

INTERVIEW (WRITTEN) Tier 3—DAP TOOL

CONTENT	• Content is accurate and thorough in detail.	0 1 2 3 4 5 6
	• Product shows complex understanding and manipulation of content.	0 1 2 3 4 5 6
	• Product shows deep probing of content.	0 1 2 3 4 5 6
	• Organization is best suited to the product.	0 1 2 3 4 5 6
PRESENTATION		
PURPOSE/ AUDIENCE	• The purpose of the interview is woven throughout each exchange. The interviewee is an expert on the topic. Ample time was given to the interviewee.	0 1 2 3 4 5 6
QUESTIONS	• Questions are exact, probing, open ended, and grammatically correct. They skillfully cover all main aspects of the topic.	0 1 2 3 4 5 6
FORMAT	• The written piece perfectly mirrors the interview in dialogue form. Any deviations are purposeful and fully explained. The introduction and conclusion cleverly enhance the purpose.	0 1 2 3 4 5 6
CREATIVITY	• Individual insight is originally expressed in relation to the content.	0 1 2 3 4 5 6
	• Individual spark is originally expressed in relation to the presentation.	0 1 2 3 4 5 6
REFLECTION	• Insightful reflection on the learning of the content through product development is expressed.	0 1 2 3 4 5 6
	• Insightful reflection on what the student learned about self as a learner is expressed.	0 1 2 3 4 5 6

Comments

_____

_____

Meaning of Performance Scale:

6—PROFESSIONAL LEVEL: level expected from a professional in the content area

5—ADVANCED LEVEL: level exceeds expectations of the standard

4—PROFICIENT LEVEL: level expected for meeting the standard

3—PROGRESSING LEVEL: level demonstrates movement toward the standard

2—NOVICE LEVEL: level demonstrates initial awareness and knowledge of standard

1—NONPERFORMING LEVEL: level indicates no effort made to meet standard

0—NONPARTICIPATING LEVEL: level indicates nothing turned in

Written Products

LETTER (BUSINESS) Tier 1—DAP TOOL

CONTENT	▪ Is the content correct and complete?	0 1 2 3 4 5 6
	▪ Has the content been thought about in a way that goes beyond a surface understanding?	0 1 2 3 4 5 6
	▪ Is the content put together in such a way that people understand it?	0 1 2 3 4 5 6
PRESENTATION		
STRUCTURE	▪ Does the letter use the correct format of return address or heading, date, inside address, salutation, body, closing, and signature block? Is the body block or indented style? Are reference initials and enclosure notations included if necessary? Is the letter free from usage, punctuation, capitalization, and spelling errors? Has correct spacing been used (such as margins)?	0 1 2 3 4 5 6
AUDIENCE, PURPOSE, AND STYLE	▪ Is the purpose stated early? Is the letter written for the expected audience and purpose? Are appropriate words used? Are the sentences varied in structure? Is a formal, respectful tone used?	0 1 2 3 4 5 6
ELABORATION AND SUPPORT	▪ Is there enough detail to support and explain the ideas? Does all information relate to the purpose? Is the letter brief?	0 1 2 3 4 5 6
CREATIVITY	▪ Is the content seen in a new way?	0 1 2 3 4 5 6
	▪ Is the presentation done in a new way?	0 1 2 3 4 5 6
REFLECTION	▪ What did you learn about the content as you completed this product?	0 1 2 3 4 5 6
	▪ What did you learn about yourself as a learner by creating this product?	0 1 2 3 4 5 6

Comments

_____

_____

Meaning of Performance Scale:

6—PROFESSIONAL LEVEL: level expected from a professional in the content area

5—ADVANCED LEVEL: level exceeds expectations of the standard

4—PROFICIENT LEVEL: level expected for meeting the standard

3—PROGRESSING LEVEL: level demonstrates movement toward the standard

2—NOVICE LEVEL: level demonstrates initial awareness and knowledge of standard

1—NONPERFORMING LEVEL: level indicates no effort made to meet standard

0—NONPARTICIPATING LEVEL: level indicates nothing turned in

LETTER (BUSINESS) Tier 2—DAP TOOL

CONTENT	▪ Content is accurate.	0 1 2 3 4 5 6
	▪ Content has depth and complexity of thought.	0 1 2 3 4 5 6
	▪ Content is organized.	0 1 2 3 4 5 6
PRESENTATION		
STRUCTURE	▪ The letter has all appropriate components: return address or heading, date, inside address, salutation, body (either block or indented), closing, and signature block. Reference initials and enclosure notations are incorporated correctly if used. The letter is free from punctuation, usage, capitalization, and spelling errors. Margins and spacing are correct.	0 1 2 3 4 5 6
AUDIENCE, PURPOSE, AND STYLE	▪ The deliberate use of varied syntax helps establish tone and purpose. Precise diction appeals to the reader and supports the purpose. A respectful, professional tone permeates the letter.	0 1 2 3 4 5 6
ELABORATION AND SUPPORT	▪ Each idea is developed and relates back to the purpose. A strong balance of general ideas and specific details creates a fluid discussion. Only pertinent support is included so that the letter is brief.	0 1 2 3 4 5 6
CREATIVITY	▪ Individual insight is expressed in relation to the content.	0 1 2 3 4 5 6
	▪ Individual spark is expressed in relation to the presentation.	0 1 2 3 4 5 6
REFLECTION	▪ Reflection on the learning of the content through product development is apparent.	0 1 2 3 4 5 6
	▪ Reflection on what the student learned about self as a learner is apparent.	0 1 2 3 4 5 6

Comments

Meaning of Performance Scale:

6—PROFESSIONAL LEVEL: level expected from a professional in the content area

5—ADVANCED LEVEL: level exceeds expectations of the standard

4—PROFICIENT LEVEL: level expected for meeting the standard

3—PROGRESSING LEVEL: level demonstrates movement toward the standard

2—NOVICE LEVEL: level demonstrates initial awareness and knowledge of standard

1—NONPERFORMING LEVEL: level indicates no effort made to meet standard

0—NONPARTICIPATING LEVEL: level indicates nothing turned in

Written Products

LETTER (BUSINESS) Tier 3—DAP TOOL

CONTENT	▪ Content is accurate and thorough in detail.	0 1 2 3 4 5 6
	▪ Product shows complex understanding and manipulation of content.	0 1 2 3 4 5 6
	▪ Product shows deep probing of content.	0 1 2 3 4 5 6
	▪ Organization is best suited to the product.	0 1 2 3 4 5 6
PRESENTATION		
STRUCTURE	▪ All appropriate components have been carefully incorporated: return address or heading, date, inside address, salutation, body (either block or indented), closing, and signature block. If needed, reference line, reference initials, enclosure notations, special mailing, and on-arrival notations are accurately included. In spite of the sophistication of the syntax, diction, and punctuation, the letter is free from errors.	0 1 2 3 4 5 6
AUDIENCE, PURPOSE, AND STYLE	▪ The purposeful use of varied syntax and powerful diction enhances audience's understanding. Courteous, professional tone clearly stems from diction, syntax, and structure. The audience and purpose dictate all aspects of the letter.	0 1 2 3 4 5 6
ELABORATION AND SUPPORT	▪ Each idea is thoroughly substantiated through pertinent detail or analyzed support. Writing anticipates readers' possible misunderstandings and handles complex ideas clearly.	0 1 2 3 4 5 6
CREATIVITY	▪ Individual insight is originally expressed in relation to the content.	0 1 2 3 4 5 6
	▪ Individual spark is originally expressed in relation to the presentation.	0 1 2 3 4 5 6
REFLECTION	▪ Insightful reflection on the learning of the content through product development is expressed.	0 1 2 3 4 5 6
	▪ Insightful reflection on what the student learned about self as a learner is expressed.	0 1 2 3 4 5 6

Comments

_____

_____

Meaning of Performance Scale:

6—PROFESSIONAL LEVEL: level expected from a professional in the content area

5—ADVANCED LEVEL: level exceeds expectations of the standard

4—PROFICIENT LEVEL: level expected for meeting the standard

3—PROGRESSING LEVEL: level demonstrates movement toward the standard

2—NOVICE LEVEL: level demonstrates initial awareness and knowledge of standard

1—NONPERFORMING LEVEL: level indicates no effort made to meet standard

0—NONPARTICIPATING LEVEL: level indicates nothing turned in

LETTER (FRIENDLY) Tier 1—DAP TOOL

CONTENT	• Is the content correct and complete?	0 1 2 3 4 5 6
	• Has the content been thought about in a way that goes beyond a surface understanding?	0 1 2 3 4 5 6
	• Is the content put together in such a way that people understand it?	0 1 2 3 4 5 6
PRESENTATION		
STRUCTURE	• Does the letter use the correct format of date, greeting, body, closing, and signature? Is the body in paragraph form? Is the letter free from usage, punctuation, capitalization, and spelling errors?	0 1 2 3 4 5 6
AUDIENCE, PURPOSE, AND STYLE	• Is the purpose stated early? Is the letter written for the expected audience and purpose? Are appropriate words used? Are the sentences varied in structure? Is the tone informal and friendly?	0 1 2 3 4 5 6
ELABORATION AND SUPPORT	• Does all information relate to the purpose? Are ideas explained and supported?	0 1 2 3 4 5 6
CREATIVITY	• Is the content seen in a new way?	0 1 2 3 4 5 6
	• Is the presentation done in a new way?	0 1 2 3 4 5 6
REFLECTION	• What did you learn about the content as you completed this product?	0 1 2 3 4 5 6
	• What did you learn about yourself as a learner by creating this product?	0 1 2 3 4 5 6

Comments

_____

_____

Meaning of Performance Scale:

6—PROFESSIONAL LEVEL: level expected from a professional in the content area

5—ADVANCED LEVEL: level exceeds expectations of the standard

4—PROFICIENT LEVEL: level expected for meeting the standard

3—PROGRESSING LEVEL: level demonstrates movement toward the standard

2—NOVICE LEVEL: level demonstrates initial awareness and knowledge of standard

1—NONPERFORMING LEVEL: level indicates no effort made to meet standard

0—NONPARTICIPATING LEVEL: level indicates nothing turned in

Written Products

LETTER (FRIENDLY) Tier 2—DAP TOOL

CONTENT	▪ Content is accurate.	0 1 2 3 4 5 6
	▪ Content has depth and complexity of thought.	0 1 2 3 4 5 6
	▪ Content is organized.	0 1 2 3 4 5 6
PRESENTATION		
STRUCTURE	▪ The letter has all appropriate components: date, greeting, body, closing, and signature. The body is written in well-developed paragraphs. The letter is free from punctuation, usage, capitalization, and spelling errors.	0 1 2 3 4 5 6
AUDIENCE, PURPOSE, AND STYLE	▪ Sentence structure and informal word choice appeal to the audience and support the purpose. A friendly, informal tone permeates the letter and establishes style.	0 1 2 3 4 5 6
ELABORATION AND SUPPORT	▪ Each idea is clearly developed. A strong balance of general ideas and specific details creates a fluid discussion.	0 1 2 3 4 5 6
CREATIVITY	▪ Individual insight is expressed in relation to the content.	0 1 2 3 4 5 6
	▪ Individual spark is expressed in relation to the presentation.	0 1 2 3 4 5 6
REFLECTION	▪ Reflection on the learning of the content through product development is apparent.	0 1 2 3 4 5 6
	▪ Reflection on what the student learned about self as a learner is apparent.	0 1 2 3 4 5 6

Comments

_____

_____

Meaning of Performance Scale:

6—PROFESSIONAL LEVEL: level expected from a professional in the content area

5—ADVANCED LEVEL: level exceeds expectations of the standard

4—PROFICIENT LEVEL: level expected for meeting the standard

3—PROGRESSING LEVEL: level demonstrates movement toward the standard

2—NOVICE LEVEL: level demonstrates initial awareness and knowledge of standard

1—NONPERFORMING LEVEL: level indicates no effort made to meet standard

0—NONPARTICIPATING LEVEL: level indicates nothing turned in

LETTER (FRIENDLY) Tier 3—DAP TOOL

CONTENT		▪ Content is accurate and thorough in detail.	0 1 2 3 4 5 6
		▪ Product shows complex understanding and manipulation of content.	0 1 2 3 4 5 6
		▪ Product shows deep probing of content.	0 1 2 3 4 5 6
		▪ Organization is best suited to the product.	0 1 2 3 4 5 6
PRESENTATION	*STRUCTURE*	▪ All appropriate components have been carefully incorporated: date, salutation, body, closing, and signature. The body is structured in well-developed paragraphs. The letter is free from errors.	0 1 2 3 4 5 6
	AUDIENCE, PURPOSE, AND STYLE	▪ Appropriate informal diction and syntax appeal to the audience and fully support the purpose. A respectful but friendly tone clearly stems from diction, syntax, and structure.	0 1 2 3 4 5 6
	ELABORATION AND SUPPORT	▪ Each idea is thoroughly substantiated through detail. Writing anticipates the reader's possible misunderstandings and handles complex ideas clearly.	0 1 2 3 4 5 6
CREATIVITY		▪ Individual insight is originally expressed in relation to the content.	0 1 2 3 4 5 6
		▪ Individual spark is originally expressed in relation to the presentation.	0 1 2 3 4 5 6
REFLECTION		▪ Insightful reflection on the learning of the content through product development is expressed.	0 1 2 3 4 5 6
		▪ Insightful reflection on what the student learned about self as a learner is expressed.	0 1 2 3 4 5 6

Comments

Meaning of Performance Scale:

6—PROFESSIONAL LEVEL: level expected from a professional in the content area

5—ADVANCED LEVEL: level exceeds expectations of the standard

4—PROFICIENT LEVEL: level expected for meeting the standard

3—PROGRESSING LEVEL: level demonstrates movement toward the standard

2—NOVICE LEVEL: level demonstrates initial awareness and knowledge of standard

1—NONPERFORMING LEVEL: level indicates no effort made to meet standard

0—NONPARTICIPATING LEVEL: level indicates nothing turned in

Written Products

SPEECH (WRITTEN) Tier 1—DAP TOOL

CONTENT	• Is the content correct and complete?	0 1 2 3 4 5 6
	• Has the content been thought about in a way that goes beyond a surface understanding?	0 1 2 3 4 5 6
	• Is the content put together in such a way that people understand it?	0 1 2 3 4 5 6
PRESENTATION		
STRUCTURE	• Does the title link to the main idea? Is an effective attention-getting device used? Is the main idea clear from the beginning? Is the speech logical in its organization, naturally flowing from one point to another? Does the speech come to a close and link back to the main idea?	0 1 2 3 4 5 6
ELABORATION AND SUPPORT	• Does all information relate to the main idea? Are ideas fully explained and supported? Is there a balance of general ideas with specific details? If quotations or other references are used, have they been used carefully and appropriately?	0 1 2 3 4 5 6
STYLE	• Is the speech developed for the expected audience and purpose? Are appropriate words used? Are the sentences varied in structure? Is a suitable tone used? Is figurative language used in an effective way?	0 1 2 3 4 5 6
CORRECTNESS	• Is the speech free from usage, punctuation, capitalization, and spelling errors? If outside sources are used, are they cited correctly?	0 1 2 3 4 5 6
CREATIVITY	• Is the content seen in a new way?	0 1 2 3 4 5 6
	• Is the presentation done in a new way?	0 1 2 3 4 5 6
REFLECTION	• What did you learn about the content as you completed this product?	0 1 2 3 4 5 6
	• What did you learn about yourself as a learner by creating this product?	0 1 2 3 4 5 6

Comments

_____

_____

Meaning of Performance Scale:

6—PROFESSIONAL LEVEL: level expected from a professional in the content area

5—ADVANCED LEVEL: level exceeds expectations of the standard

4—PROFICIENT LEVEL: level expected for meeting the standard

3—PROGRESSING LEVEL: level demonstrates movement toward the standard

2—NOVICE LEVEL: level demonstrates initial awareness and knowledge of standard

1—NONPERFORMING LEVEL: level indicates no effort made to meet standard

0—NONPARTICIPATING LEVEL: level indicates nothing turned in

Assessing Differentiated Student Products © Prufrock Press • This page may be photocopied or reproduced with permission for classroom use.

SPEECH (WRITTEN) Tier 2—DAP TOOL

CONTENT	▪ Content is accurate.	0 1 2 3 4 5 6
	▪ Content has depth and complexity of thought.	0 1 2 3 4 5 6
	▪ Content is organized.	0 1 2 3 4 5 6
PRESENTATION		
STRUCTURE	▪ Title enhances the speech. The attention-getting device clearly gains the audience's interest. The main idea is clear and well developed. Strong transitions between main points link to the purpose and any narrative threads. The speech is logical in its organization. The conclusion, pulling together all aspects, comes to a strong closure.	0 1 2 3 4 5 6
ELABORATION AND SUPPORT	▪ Each idea is fully developed and relates to the purpose. A strong balance of general ideas and specific details creates a fluid discussion. Quotations or other references, if used, fully elaborate on or support the main points and are smoothly incorporated.	0 1 2 3 4 5 6
STYLE	▪ The purposeful use of varied syntax and precise diction aids in the reader's understanding. Tone is consistent to purpose. Voice clearly stems from diction, syntax, and figurative language. Ethos is strongly realized in the audience.	0 1 2 3 4 5 6
CORRECTNESS	▪ The speech is free from punctuation, usage, capitalization, and spelling errors. Outside sources are cited correctly.	0 1 2 3 4 5 6
CREATIVITY	▪ Individual insight is expressed in relation to the content.	0 1 2 3 4 5 6
	▪ Individual spark is expressed in relation to the presentation.	0 1 2 3 4 5 6
REFLECTION	▪ Reflection on the learning of the content through product development is apparent.	0 1 2 3 4 5 6
	▪ Reflection on what the student learned about self as a learner is apparent.	0 1 2 3 4 5 6

Comments

_____

_____

Meaning of Performance Scale:

6—PROFESSIONAL LEVEL: level expected from a professional in the content area

5—ADVANCED LEVEL: level exceeds expectations of the standard

4—PROFICIENT LEVEL: level expected for meeting the standard

3—PROGRESSING LEVEL: level demonstrates movement toward the standard

2—NOVICE LEVEL: level demonstrates initial awareness and knowledge of standard

1—NONPERFORMING LEVEL: level indicates no effort made to meet standard

0—NONPARTICIPATING LEVEL: level indicates nothing turned in

SPEECH (WRITTEN) Tier 3—DAP TOOL

CONTENT		▪ Content is accurate and thorough in detail.	0 1 2 3 4 5 6
		▪ Product shows complex understanding and manipulation of content.	0 1 2 3 4 5 6
		▪ Product shows deep probing of content.	0 1 2 3 4 5 6
		▪ Organization is best suited to the product.	0 1 2 3 4 5 6
PRESENTATION			
	STRUCTURE	▪ Title reflects the purpose. The attention-getting device cleverly and uniquely gains the audience's interest and provides a thoughtful transition to the thesis. The original and creative thesis guides the entire speech with a coherent, narrative thread. Sophisticated transitions subtly link all aspects. Secondary arguments fully develop key concepts or ideas critical to the purpose. The speech is ideally organized. Conclusion emphasizes pertinent information. The significance of the conclusion is clear.	0 1 2 3 4 5 6
	ELABORATION AND SUPPORT	▪ Each idea is thoroughly substantiated through pertinent detail or analyzed support from a variety of sources. Pertinent quotations and other references fully elaborate on or support the idea; their inclusion is seamless. The speech anticipates audience's possible misunderstandings and handles complex ideas clearly.	0 1 2 3 4 5 6
	STYLE	▪ The purposeful use of varied syntax and powerful diction enhances the audience's understanding. Tone clearly stems from diction, syntax, and figurative language. Effective rhetorical devices emphasize thesis.	0 1 2 3 4 5 6
	CORRECTNESS	▪ In spite of the complexity of the syntax, diction, and punctuation, the speech is free from errors. Outside sources are cited correctly.	0 1 2 3 4 5 6
CREATIVITY		▪ Individual insight is originally expressed in relation to the content.	0 1 2 3 4 5 6
		▪ Individual spark is originally expressed in relation to the presentation.	0 1 2 3 4 5 6
REFLECTION		▪ Insightful reflection on the learning of the content through product development is expressed.	0 1 2 3 4 5 6
		▪ Insightful reflection on what the student learned about self as a learner is expressed.	0 1 2 3 4 5 6

Comments

_____

_____

Meaning of Performance Scale:

6—PROFESSIONAL LEVEL: level expected from a professional in the content area

5—ADVANCED LEVEL: level exceeds expectations of the standard

4—PROFICIENT LEVEL: level expected for meeting the standard

3—PROGRESSING LEVEL: level demonstrates movement toward the standard

2—NOVICE LEVEL: level demonstrates initial awareness and knowledge of standard

1—NONPERFORMING LEVEL: level indicates no effort made to meet standard

0—NONPARTICIPATING LEVEL: level indicates nothing turned in

TECHNICAL REPORT Tier 1—DAP TOOL

CONTENT	▪ Is the content correct and complete?	0 1 2 3 4 5 6
	▪ Has the content been thought about in a way that goes beyond a surface understanding?	0 1 2 3 4 5 6
	▪ Is the content put together in such a way that people understand it?	0 1 2 3 4 5 6
PRESENTATION		
FORM	▪ Does the title describe the main idea? Is the topic clearly stated early in the paper? Do strong transitions lead from one section to another? Does each section have one main idea? Does it come to a close and link back to the topic?	0 1 2 3 4 5 6
DETAIL	▪ Is there enough detail to prove the points? Does all information relate to the main idea? Are the ideas fully explained and supported? Are all figures and graphs explained well?	0 1 2 3 4 5 6
STYLE	▪ Is it written for the expected audience? Are the words clear and concise? Has slang been avoided and all jargon explained? Are the sentences straightforward and clear? Is it written in active voice and third person? Are tables used to organize data when appropriate?	0 1 2 3 4 5 6
LAYOUT	▪ Do headings help the audience understand the upcoming section? Are important diagrams, charts, illustrations, or tables included and explained? Are units included with all data? Is the layout consistent as to font, bullets, underlining, and so forth?	0 1 2 3 4 5 6
CREATIVITY	▪ Is the content seen in a new way?	0 1 2 3 4 5 6
	▪ Is the presentation done in a new way?	0 1 2 3 4 5 6
REFLECTION	▪ What did you learn about the content as you completed this product?	0 1 2 3 4 5 6
	▪ What did you learn about yourself as a learner by creating this product?	0 1 2 3 4 5 6

Comments

_____

_____

Meaning of Performance Scale:

6—PROFESSIONAL LEVEL: level expected from a professional in the content area

5—ADVANCED LEVEL: level exceeds expectations of the standard

4—PROFICIENT LEVEL: level expected for meeting the standard

3—PROGRESSING LEVEL: level demonstrates movement toward the standard

2—NOVICE LEVEL: level demonstrates initial awareness and knowledge of standard

1—NONPERFORMING LEVEL: level indicates no effort made to meet standard

0—NONPARTICIPATING LEVEL: level indicates nothing turned in

Note. Adapted from *Strategies for Differentiating Instruction: Best Practices for the Classroom* (p. 211), by J. L. Roberts and T. F. Inman, 2007, Waco, TX: Prufrock Press. Copyright © 2007 by Prufrock Press. Adapted with permission.

Written Products

TECHNICAL REPORT Tier 2—DAP TOOL

CONTENT	• Content is accurate.	0 1 2 3 4 5 6
	• Content has depth and complexity of thought.	0 1 2 3 4 5 6
	• Content is organized.	0 1 2 3 4 5 6
PRESENTATION		
FORM	• Title enhances the writing. The thesis of the writing is clear and immediate. Transitions between sections link to the purpose. Each section develops an idea critical to the purpose. The conclusion pulls together all aspects of the writing and clearly links to the thesis.	0 1 2 3 4 5 6
DETAIL	• Each idea is fully developed and relates back to the purpose of the writing. Possible questions of the readers are addressed. The writing clearly relates to the figures and graphs presented. Graphs are used to illustrate trends in data.	0 1 2 3 4 5 6
STYLE	• The straightforward, clear syntax aids in the audience's understanding. Precise and economical word choice appeals to audience and supports purpose. Ambiguity is avoided. Tone is consistent to purpose. Abstract ideas are carefully explained. Active voice and third person are used.	0 1 2 3 4 5 6
LAYOUT	• The layout clarifies the meaning through appropriate headings and labeling that specifically prepare the reader for the upcoming content. Illustrations, diagrams, charts, and/or tables simplify the explanation of complex ideas and are well placed. The layout is consistent as to font, bullets, underlining, and so forth, so that the document presents a unified, coherent impression to the reader.	0 1 2 3 4 5 6
CREATIVITY	• Individual insight is expressed in relation to the content.	0 1 2 3 4 5 6
	• Individual spark is expressed in relation to the presentation.	0 1 2 3 4 5 6
REFLECTION	• Reflection on the learning of the content through product development is apparent.	0 1 2 3 4 5 6
	• Reflection on what the student learned about self as a learner is apparent.	0 1 2 3 4 5 6

Comments

_____

_____

Meaning of Performance Scale:

6—PROFESSIONAL LEVEL: level expected from a professional in the content area

5—ADVANCED LEVEL: level exceeds expectations of the standard

4—PROFICIENT LEVEL: level expected for meeting the standard

3—PROGRESSING LEVEL: level demonstrates movement toward the standard

2—NOVICE LEVEL: level demonstrates initial awareness and knowledge of standard

1—NONPERFORMING LEVEL: level indicates no effort made to meet standard

0—NONPARTICIPATING LEVEL: level indicates nothing turned in

Note. Adapted from *Strategies for Differentiating Instruction: Best Practices for the Classroom* (p. 212), by J. L. Roberts and T. F. Inman, 2007, Waco, TX: Prufrock Press. Copyright © 2007 by Prufrock Press. Adapted with permission.

TECHNICAL REPORT Tier 3—DAP TOOL

CONTENT		
	▪ Content is accurate and thorough in detail.	0 1 2 3 4 5 6
	▪ Product shows complex understanding and manipulation of content.	0 1 2 3 4 5 6
	▪ Product shows deep probing of content.	0 1 2 3 4 5 6
	▪ Organization is best suited to the product.	0 1 2 3 4 5 6
PRESENTATION		
FORM	▪ Title reflects purpose. The thesis is immediately clear, and the writing is focused. Transitions subtly link all aspects together. Sections fully develop key concepts or ideas critical to the purpose. Conclusion refers back to the purpose of the document and summarizes pertinent knowledge and information. The significance of the conclusion is explained.	0 1 2 3 4 5 6
DETAIL	▪ Each idea is thoroughly substantiated through pertinent detail or analyzed support. Writing anticipates readers' possible misunderstandings and handles complex ideas clearly. Strong, elaborate support proves points. Only pertinent information is included. The reader is clearly directed to figures and graphs for validation of ideas within the text. How variables were handled is explained.	0 1 2 3 4 5 6
STYLE	▪ The straightforward syntax clearly enhances purpose. Diction is precise, economical, and succinct to avoid ambiguity. Tone consistently maintains the audience's attention. Concrete images clarify abstract ideas. Active voice and third person are used skillfully.	0 1 2 3 4 5 6
LAYOUT	▪ Purposeful manipulation of layout enhances understanding through carefully selected headings. The format is highly consistent as to font, bullets, underlining, and so forth, so that a professional, unified impression is presented to the reader. Illustrations, diagrams, charts, or tables develop and/or explain complex ideas fully. Placement enhances understanding.	0 1 2 3 4 5 6
CREATIVITY	▪ Individual insight is originally expressed in relation to the content.	0 1 2 3 4 5 6
	▪ Individual spark is originally expressed in relation to the presentation.	0 1 2 3 4 5 6
REFLECTION	▪ Insightful reflection on the learning of the content through product development is expressed.	0 1 2 3 4 5 6
	▪ Insightful reflection on what the student learned about self as a learner is expressed.	0 1 2 3 4 5 6

Comments

_____

_____

Meaning of Performance Scale:

6—PROFESSIONAL LEVEL: level expected from a professional in the content area

5—ADVANCED LEVEL: level exceeds expectations of the standard

4—PROFICIENT LEVEL: level expected for meeting the standard

3—PROGRESSING LEVEL: level demonstrates movement toward the standard

2—NOVICE LEVEL: level demonstrates initial awareness and knowledge of standard

1—NONPERFORMING LEVEL: level indicates no effort made to meet standard

0—NONPARTICIPATING LEVEL: level indicates nothing turned in

Note. Adapted from *Strategies for Differentiating Instruction: Best Practices for the Classroom* (p. 213), by J. L. Roberts and T. F. Inman, 2007, Waco, TX: Prufrock Press. Copyright © 2007 by Prufrock Press. Adapted with permission.

Written Products

Chapter 7

Getting Started With the DAP Tool

Now that you have read about the DAP Tool—its components, Performance Scale, tiers, and ways to implement it—think about how you can put it to use in your own classroom or school. The sooner you start, the sooner you simplify assessment, encourage differentiation, and remove the learning ceiling.

As Easy as 1, 2, 3 . . .

1. Once you've embraced the protocol, you need to share it with your students. Teach the DAP Tool and its three main innovations: four components, seven-level Performance Scale, and three tiers. Depending on your class, you may want to begin with a focus on the components and scale.

2. When introducing the Performance Scale, be sure to provide definitions of the standards. Ideally, this would include sample products depicting each level. Also address how you will transfer the scale into a grade. (Remember that this can work in a variety of ways—you're the one in control of implementation.)

3. The DAP Tool is printed in a size that you can readily duplicate. Decide how you will store this in your room: file cabinet, computer, or even a DAP Tool Drawer. The idea is to provide DAP Tools for myriad products, thus encouraging self-expression, creativity, own-

ership—all of the concepts that have been threaded throughout the book.

4. If you want to use products that don't have a DAP Tool already created, Figures 7.1, 7.2, and 7.3 are templates for each tier. All you need to do is develop the Presentation section for that product. Remember that three of the components—Content, Creativity, and Reflection—remain the same at each of the tier levels for all DAP Tools. Once you have become familiar with the protocol offered by the DAP Tool, you will find that you can create the Presentation section for other products. Some of your students may even surprise you with their ability and willingness to create DAP Tools.

5. Don't get discouraged. Keep in mind that the first time you try something you seldom will do as well as you do the next (and subsequent) time you implement it. As one teacher said: "The next time I use the DAP Tool, I know that the students will know more about what to expect because I will know more about what to expect. That first step is always the toughest." It takes time for you and your students to internalize the DAP Tool.

Teachers have had students work on products, often calling them *projects*, for a long time. Therefore, products for classroom assignments are not new. However, developing scoring guides for each product option in each assignment is cumbersome. The DAP Tool offers several dimensions that facilitate using products routinely and guide the students toward the development of high-level products.

What are the unique dimensions of the DAP Tool?

- Foremost is the fact that the DAP Tool provides a protocol for product assessment that can be used at all grade levels and in all content areas. It establishes both the vocabulary for students as they are developing high-level products and also for teachers as they assess the products. This tool epitomizes formative assessment.

- The DAP Tool offers a ready instrument for differentiating instruction for students of varying levels of ability, experience, interest, and readiness levels. Its availability is a tremendous asset to teachers who want to differentiate but who become bogged down with the additional time taken to design scoring guides at varying levels for different assignments.

- The DAP Tool serves as preassessment in regard to all four of the components: Content, Presentation, Creativity, and Reflection. The results feed information to the teacher and the student about the learning

Tier 1—DAP TOOL

CONTENT	▪ Is the content correct and complete?	0 1 2 3 4 5 6
	▪ Has the content been thought about in a way that goes beyond a surface understanding?	0 1 2 3 4 5 6
	▪ Is the content put together in such a way that people understand it?	0 1 2 3 4 5 6
PRESENTATION		0 1 2 3 4 5 6
		0 1 2 3 4 5 6
		0 1 2 3 4 5 6
		0 1 2 3 4 5 6
CREATIVITY	▪ Is the content seen in a new way?	0 1 2 3 4 5 6
	▪ Is the presentation done in a new way?	0 1 2 3 4 5 6
REFLECTION	▪ What did you learn about the content as you completed this product?	0 1 2 3 4 5 6
	▪ What did you learn about yourself as a learner by creating this product?	0 1 2 3 4 5 6

Comments

_____

_____

Meaning of Performance Scale:

6—PROFESSIONAL LEVEL: level expected from a professional in the content area

5—ADVANCED LEVEL: level exceeds expectations of the standard

4—PROFICIENT LEVEL: level expected for meeting the standard

3—PROGRESSING LEVEL: level demonstrates movement toward the standard

2—NOVICE LEVEL: level demonstrates initial awareness and knowledge of standard

1—NONPERFORMING LEVEL: level indicates no effort made to meet standard

0—NONPARTICIPATING LEVEL: level indicates nothing turned in

Figure 7.1. Tier 1 template.

Note. Adapted from *Strategies for Differentiating Instruction: Best Practices for the Classroom,* by J. L. Roberts and T. F. Inman, 2007, Waco, TX: Prufrock Press. Copyright © 2007 by Prufrock Press. Adapted with permission.

Tier 2—DAP TOOL

CONTENT		
	▪ Content is accurate.	0 1 2 3 4 5 6
	▪ Content has depth and complexity of thought.	0 1 2 3 4 5 6
	▪ Content is organized.	0 1 2 3 4 5 6

PRESENTATION		
		0 1 2 3 4 5 6
		0 1 2 3 4 5 6
		0 1 2 3 4 5 6
		0 1 2 3 4 5 6

CREATIVITY		
	▪ Individual insight is expressed in relation to the content.	0 1 2 3 4 5 6
	▪ Individual spark is expressed in relation to the presentation.	0 1 2 3 4 5 6

REFLECTION		
	▪ Reflection on the learning of the content through product development is apparent.	0 1 2 3 4 5 6
	▪ Reflection on what the student learned about self as a learner is apparent.	0 1 2 3 4 5 6

Comments

_____

_____

Meaning of Performance Scale:

6—PROFESSIONAL LEVEL: level expected from a professional in the content area

5—ADVANCED LEVEL: level exceeds expectations of the standard

4—PROFICIENT LEVEL: level expected for meeting the standard

3—PROGRESSING LEVEL: level demonstrates movement toward the standard

2—NOVICE LEVEL: level demonstrates initial awareness and knowledge of standard

1—NONPERFORMING LEVEL: level indicates no effort made to meet standard

0—NONPARTICIPATING LEVEL: level indicates nothing turned in

Figure 7.2. Tier 2 template.

Note. Adapted from *Strategies for Differentiating Instruction: Best Practices for the Classroom,* by J. L. Roberts and T. F. Inman, 2007, Waco, TX: Prufrock Press. Copyright © 2007 by Prufrock Press. Adapted with permission.

Tier 3—DAP TOOL

CONTENT		
	▪ Content is accurate and thorough in detail.	0 1 2 3 4 5 6
	▪ Product shows complex understanding and manipulation of content.	0 1 2 3 4 5 6
	▪ Product shows deep probing of content.	0 1 2 3 4 5 6
	▪ Organization is best suited to the product.	0 1 2 3 4 5 6
PRESENTATION		0 1 2 3 4 5 6
		0 1 2 3 4 5 6
		0 1 2 3 4 5 6
		0 1 2 3 4 5 6
CREATIVITY	▪ Individual insight is originally expressed in relation to the content.	0 1 2 3 4 5 6
	▪ Individual spark is originally expressed in relation to the presentation.	0 1 2 3 4 5 6
REFLECTION	▪ Insightful reflection on the learning of the content through product development is expressed.	0 1 2 3 4 5 6
	▪ Insightful reflection on what the student learned about self as a learner is expressed.	0 1 2 3 4 5 6

Comments

_____

_____

Meaning of Performance Scale:

6—PROFESSIONAL LEVEL: level expected from a professional in the content area

5—ADVANCED LEVEL: level exceeds expectations of the standard

4—PROFICIENT LEVEL: level expected for meeting the standard

3—PROGRESSING LEVEL: level demonstrates movement toward the standard

2—NOVICE LEVEL: level demonstrates initial awareness and knowledge of standard

1—NONPERFORMING LEVEL: level indicates no effort made to meet standard

0—NONPARTICIPATING LEVEL: level indicates nothing turned in

Figure 7.3. Tier 3 template.

Note. Adapted from *Strategies for Differentiating Instruction: Best Practices for the Classroom,* by J. L. Roberts and T. F. Inman, 2007, Waco, TX: Prufrock Press. Copyright © 2007 by Prufrock Press. Adapted with permission.

that occurred during the development of the product. This information dictates the next steps for learning.

- The DAP Tool establishes a seven-level Performance Scale that removes the learning ceiling. This scale removes barriers to learning as it opens opportunities for students to produce high-level products, even at the level that characterizes professionals in a field who use the specific product.

- The DAP Tool provides the professional level that makes students aware that professionals use products in their fields and that professionals make those products at a level that is rarely seen in school; however, including the professional level inserts a level that students can strive to reach.

- The introduction of learning styles categorized as *PRIMARYsecondary* expands which learning preferences might be addressed. This encourages exploration and increases motivation.

- In terms of highlighting 21st-century skills, the DAP Tool is forward looking. Creativity and Reflection are staples in the DAP Tool along with the Content and the Presentation.

Ultimately your goal as a teacher is to produce young people who are lifelong learners, individuals who can be successful as they transition to postsecondary opportunities and eventually to careers. The 21st century is making demands of its citizens—demands that require a wide range of skills and knowledge. The goal of project-based learning is not the earning of a grade but rather the preparation of young people for the future. The DAP Tool can be used to facilitate students being prepared for what lies ahead—not with the answers but with the skills.

Developing lifelong learners is the lofty goal of schooling, one that doesn't happen overnight. Yet this is the goal that must be met if the young person is to be successful in a variety of opportunities that follow high school. "For teachers to be effective in supporting student learning they must constantly be checking for student understanding. Moreover, they must convey to students the importance of students themselves taking responsibility for reflecting on and monitoring their own learning progress" (Chappius et al., 2005, p. 276). "Engaging students in critiquing their own work serves both cognitive and motivational purposes. Ultimately the habit of self-assessment leads to the self-monitoring of performance . . ." (Shepard et al., 2005, p. 291). Teachers and students working together can reach this lofty goal. Ultimately, the student has to take charge of his own learning if he is to become a lifelong learner. During the 13 years of schooling between kindergarten and high school graduation, teachers play a tremendous role in facilitating young people taking charge of their own learning—or in not doing so.

Now just get started. You will win, and so will your students as they are challenged to learn at higher levels on an ongoing basis.

References

Adams, K. (2006). *The sources of innovation and creation.* Retrieved March 13, 2008, from http://www.skillscommission.org/pdf/commissioned_papers/Sources%20of%20Innovation%20and%20Creativity.pdf

Anderson, L. W., Krathwohl, D. R., Airasian, P. W., Cruikshank, K. A., Mayer, R. E., Pintrich, P. R., et al. (Eds.). (2001). *A taxonomy for learning, teaching, and assessing: A revision of Bloom's taxonomy of educational objectives* (Abridged ed.). New York: Longman.

Arter, J. A., & McTighe, J. (2001). *Scoring rubrics in the classroom: Using performance criteria for assessing and improving student performance.* Thousand Oaks, CA: Corwin Press.

Bernstein, A. (2007, October 30). Why the United States needs an innovation strategy. *strategy+business.* Retrieved March 12, 2008, from http://www.strategy-business.com/li/leadingideas/li00049?pg=0

Bloom, B. S. (Ed.). (1956). *Taxonomy of educational objectives: The classification of educational goals. Handbook I: Cognitive domain.* New York: Longman.

Chappius, S., Stiggins, R. J., Arter, J., & Chappius, J. (2005). *Assessment for learning: An action guide for school leaders.* Portland, OR: Educational Testing Service.

Coil, C. (2004). *Standards-based activities and assessments for the differentiated classroom.* Marion, IL: Pieces of Learning.

Curry, J., & Samara, J. (1991). *Product guide kit: The curriculum project.* Austin, TX: Curriculum Project.

Dunn, R., & Dunn, K. (2003). *Dunn and Dunn learning style models.* Retrieved February 28, 2008, from http://www.learningstyles.net

Fishman, T. C. (2006). *China, inc.: How the rise of the next superpower challenges America and the world.* New York: Scribner.

Florida, R. (2005). *The flight of the creative class: The new global competition for talent.* New York: HarperBusiness.

Friedman, T. L. (2007). *The world is flat 3.0: A brief history of the twenty-first century.* New York: Picodor.

Kao, J. (2007). *Innovation nation: How America is losing its innovation edge, why it matters, and what we can do to get it back.* New York: Free Press.

Karnes, F., & Stephens, K. (2000). *The ultimate guide for student product development and evaluation.* Waco, TX: Prufrock Press.

Lamarche-Bisson, D. (2002, September). Learning styles—What are they? How can they help? *World and I, 17,* 268.

Lazear, D. (1998). *The rubrics way: Using multiple intelligences to assess understanding.* Tucson, AZ: Zephyr Press.

Partnership for 21st Century Skills. (2007). *The intellectual and policy foundations of the 21st century skills framework.* Retrieved April 1, 2008, from http://www.21stcenturyskills.org/route21/images/stories/epapers/skills_foundations_final.pdf

Roberts, J. L., & Inman, T. F. (2007). *Strategies for differentiating instruction: Best practices for the classroom.* Waco, TX: Prufrock Press.

Sanders, W. L. (1998, December). Value-added assessment. *School Administrator, 55,* 24–27.

Shepard, L., Hammerness, K., Darling-Hammond, L., Rust, F., Snowden, J. B., Gordon, E., et al. (2005). Assessment. In L. Darling-Hammond & J. Bransford (Eds.), *Preparing teachers for a changing world: What teachers should learn and be able to do* (pp. 275–326). San Francisco: Jossey-Bass.

Silver, H. F., Strong, R. W., & Perini, M. J. (2000). *So each may learn: Integrating learning styles & multiple intelligences.* Alexandria, VA: Association for Supervision and Curriculum Development.

Stiggins, R. J. (2002, June 6). Assessment crisis: The absence of assessment for learning. *Phi Delta Kappan.* Retrieved April 15, 2008, from http://electronicportfolios.org/afl/Stiggins-AssessmentCrisis.pdf

Task Force on the Future of American Innovation. (2005). *The knowledge economy: Is the United States losing its competitive edge?* Retrieved March 12, 2008, from http://www.futureofinnovation.org/PDF/Benchmarks.pdf

Torrance, E. P. (1963). *Education and the creative potential.* Minneapolis: University of Minnesota Press.

The United States Commission on National Security/21st Century. (2001, February 15). *Road map for national security: Imperative for change.* Retrieved April 1, 2008, from http://govinfo.library.unt.edu/nssg/PhaseIIIFR.pdf

VARK: Visual study strategies. (2007). Retrieved March 5, 2008, from http://www.vark-learn.com/english/page.asp?p=visual

Vincent, A., & Ross, D. (2001). Personalize training: Determine learning styles, personality types and multiple intelligences online. *The Learning Organization, 8*(1), 36.

Vygotsky, L. S. (1978). *Mind in society: The development of higher psychological processes.* Cambridge, MA: Harvard University Press.

Webb, N. L. (1999). *Alignment of science and mathematics standards and assessments in four states* (Research Monograph No. 18). Madison, WI: National Institute for Science Education.

Winebrenner, S. (2001). *Teaching gifted kids in the regular classroom.* Minneapolis, MN: Free Spirit.

Zapalska, A., & Brozik, D. (2006). Learning styles and online education. *Campus-Wide Information Systems, 23,* 325–335.

Appendix A:
PRIMARYsecondary Learning Styles for Products List

Kinesthetic

- Collection
  K, Kv, or Kvw
- Costume
  K, Kv (or if only designing, V)
- Dance
  K
- Demonstration
  K, Ko, or Kwo
- Diorama
  Kv or Kvw
- Dramatic Presentation
  Ko or Kow
- Experiment
  K or Kw
- Game
  Kw or Kvw
- Invention
  Kw or Kwv
- Mask
  Kv or Kvw
- Mentorship
  Ko, Kt, or Kw
- Mime
  K

- Mock Trial (attorney)
  Kov
- Mock Trial (defendant)
  Kov
- Mock Trial (judge)
  Kov
- Mock Trial (plaintiff)
  Kov
- Model
  Kv
- Musical
  Ko or Kwo (or if only writing, W)
- Painting
  Kv
- Play
  Ko or Kwo (or if only writing, W)
- Project
  Kvw
- Puppet
  Kv
- Puppet Show
  Kvw or Kvwo
- Science Fair Project
  Kvw
- Sculpture
  Kv

- Service Learning Project
  K or Kw
- Skit
  K or Kw

Oral

- Advertisement (radio)
  O or Ow
- Audiotape
  O or Ow
- Choral Reading
  O, Ow, or Owk
- Debate
  O, Ow, or Owk
- Dialogue
  O or Ow
- Interview (live)
  O or Ow
- Interview (recorded)
  O or Ow
- Monologue
  Ok or Owk
- Newscast
  Ok or Owk
- Oral Report/Presentation
  O, Ow, or Owk
- PSA (radio)
  O or Ow
- Song
  O, Ow, or Owk
- Speech (oral)
  O, Ow, or Owk
- Story Telling
  O, Ok, or Owk

Technological

- Advertisement (television)
  Tv
- Blog
  Tvw

- Computer Graphic
  Tv
- Computer Program
  Tw
- Documentary
  Tw (script) or Twovk
- Movie
  Tw (script) or Twovk
- Podcast
  Tw or Twv
- PowerPoint Presentation
  Twv
- PSA (television)
  Tv, Tvw, Tvwo, or Tvwok
- Video Game
  Tvw or Tvwo
- Web Page
  Tvw
- Wiki
  Tv

Visual

- Advertisement/PSA (print)
  V or Vw
- Blueprint
  V, Vw, or Vwt
- Book Cover
  Vw or Vwt
- Bulletin Board
  V or Vw
- Cartoon
  V or Vw
- Chart
  Vw or Vwt
- Collage
  V or Vw
- Diagram
  Vw or Vwt
- Drawing
  V
- Exhibit/Display
  Vwk or Vwkt

- Graph
  Vw
- Graphic Organizer
  Vw or Vwt
- Illustration
  V
- Mural
  V
- Museum Exhibit
  Vwk or Vwkt
- Pamphlet/Brochure
  Vw or Vwt
- Photo
  V or Vt
- Photo Essay
  Vw or Vwt
- Political Cartoon
  Vw
- Poster
  Vw
- Scrapbook
  V or Vw
- Venn Diagram
  Vw

Written

- Biography
  W, Wv, or Wvt
- Book
  W, Wv, or Wvt
- Case Study
  W or Wv
- Column
  W
- Diary/Journal
  W
- Document-Based Question
  W
- Editorial
  W
- Essay
  W

- Feature Article
  W or Wv
- Greeting Card
  Wv or Wvt
- Illustrated Story
  Wv or Wvt
- Interview (written)
  W or Wo
- Lesson
  W
- Letter (business)
  W
- Letter (friendly)
  W
- Letter to Editor
  W
- Newsletter
  W, Wv, or Wvt
- Newspaper Article
  W or Wv
- Open Response
  W
- Outline
  W
- Plan
  W or Wv
- Poem
  W or Wv
- Questionnaire
  W or Wo
- Research Report
  W
- Review
  W or Wv
- Script
  W
- Speech (written)
  W
- Story
  W or Wo
- Survey
  W or Wo
- Technical Report
  W or Wv

- Timeline
  Wv or Wvt
- Written Report
  W

About the Authors

Julia Link Roberts is the Mahurin Professor of Gifted Studies at Western Kentucky University. She serves as Executive Director of The Center for Gifted Studies and the Carol Martin Gatton Academy of Mathematics and Science in Kentucky. Dr. Roberts is a member of the board of directors for the National Association for Gifted Children and the Kentucky Association for Gifted Education, and she is an appointed member of the Kentucky Advisory Council for Gifted and Talented Education. Dr. Roberts directs programming for young people in the summer and on Saturdays and provides professional development for educators across the country. She and Tracy Inman coauthored *Strategies for Differentiating Instruction: Best Practices for the Classroom* (2007). The two also write an advocacy column for *Parenting for High Potential*.

Tracy Ford Inman has devoted her career to meeting the needs of young people, especially those who are gifted and talented. She has taught at both the high school and collegiate levels as well as in summer programs for gifted and talented youth. This Who's Who Among American Educators teacher was a Kentucky Teacher of the Year semifinalist in 1992. She now serves as Associate Director of The Center for Gifted Studies at Western Kentucky University in Bowling Green, KY. Mrs. Inman has presented at the state, national, and international levels, trained hundreds of teachers in differentiation strategies, published multiple articles, and served as writer/editor for the award-winning newsmagazine for The Center for Gifted Studies, *The Challenge*.